TRUTHS *that*
TRANSFORM

GREAT TRUTHS TO TOUCH AND TRANSFORM YOUR LIFE

STUDY GUIDE

CORAL RIDGE
MINISTRIES
Dr. D. James Kennedy, Founder

Coral Ridge Ministries
Post Office Box 1920
Fort Lauderdale, Florida 33302-1920
1-800-988-7884
www.coralridge.org
letters@coralridge.org

Contents

Introduction

"SODA FIZZ" OR "ETERNAL VERITIES"?

In *Truths That Transform*, Dr. D. James Kennedy addressed the need he saw for the Christian Church to return to "the eternal verities of God's Word" in an age of "soda fizz theology." Most of us wouldn't say "soda fizz" and "theology" in the same breath! Yet, when he originally wrote this book, Dr. Kennedy recognized that many Christians had little interest in the meatier subjects of Christian doctrine. The evidence shows that this may be even truer today. People have a taste for hearing about a loving God, but they have no spiritual appetite for learning about God's holiness. They are interested in what God can do for them, but not what God requires of us. In fact, researchers have found that this is conspicuously the case with teens and young adults. It is commonplace for many students who claim to be Christians to hold beliefs that are far from biblical, orthodox Christianity. Some have termed these beliefs a kind of "moralistic therapeutic deism,"[1] which claims that the point of faith is to "be good, to feel good, and to have a God to always call on for help without expecting anything in return."[2]

If you are searching for study material that will aid you in developing a firm foundation of biblical truth in the face of relativism, this study guide will help you do just that. The "eternal verities" presented in *Truths That Transform* will not necessarily make you "feel good." They may challenge you to reflect on your current beliefs and to change some of your views about what you consider to be "biblical truths." As you work through these chapters, in what many consider to be Dr. Kennedy's foundational book, you will find that his clear explanations of these great truths will deepen your understanding of biblical doctrine. The chapters will answer fundamental questions that may still trouble you; such as: "Is God in control of everything?" "Does God really care whether I live or die?" "What makes Christ unique?" and "How can I know that I am a Christian?" All of these topics are handled with clarity and brevity. Even those who have a background in theology find Dr. Kennedy's writings on these topics refreshing and stimulating. But, for the young believer, they are gold. You will be grounded in your understanding of the historic Christian faith in a way that is rarely matched.

BE READY WITH THE TRUTH

One of Dr. Kennedy's greatest strengths as a communicator was his ability to present difficult ideas in a clear and cogent way. He consistently handled complex issues in a way that went straight to the heart of the matter. His arguments in support of biblical truth and his refutations of unbiblical teaching are masterful examples to all who would teach the truth and confront lies in our society. Any effort you invest into understanding and applying what he wrote will be richly rewarded. Mastering *Truths That Transform* should equip you to "always be ready to give a defense to everyone who asks you a reason for the hope that is in you" (1 Peter 3:15), regardless of where or to whom you are speaking.

The chapter questions in this study guide will help you to achieve a deeper understanding of these "great truths of the historic Christian faith" by guiding you through Dr. Kennedy's explanations of them. You will also see how he demonstrates the biblical basis for each truth, as well as the arguments he gives against those who disbelieve them. But this study guide is not intended to be just an "intellectual exercise." As you learn these truths, you will also be invited to think of how and where you might apply them. You should also find that after completing this study you have increased your ability to explain to others these important doctrines, which are the biblical and theological foundations of our Christian faith.

MAXIMIZE YOUR LEARNING

You might think of this study guide as your "tour guide" through the material in *Truths That Transform*. Like a guide, it will show you points of interest and explain their meaning and significance. It will move you along a directed path in your reading of the book. By following its guidance, you will maximize your learning of these biblical truths.

The chapter introductions begin by pointing to the context of the chapter topic in contemporary culture. As you read them, think of your own experiences or those of others which may further illustrate the importance of the chapter topic.

The learning objectives identify what you can expect to learn through your study of the chapter. These objectives can serve as prompts for a self-review of the material. After completing the chapter study, return to these objectives and phrase each one as a question and see if you can provide the answers.

There are three types, or "levels," of questions for each chapter. By considering the purpose of each type of question, you will be able to respond more thoughtfully to them.

> **LEVEL ONE QUESTIONS** will help you identify Dr. Kennedy's key points and understand his specific arguments in regard to the chapter's topic. These questions will assist you in gaining a deeper personal understanding of the fundamental Christian doctrines and truths presented in relation to the topic.
> **LEVEL TWO QUESTIONS** will challenge you to consider how the chapter content connects with your personal situation or that of your church or community. These questions will prompt you to think more deeply about the personal application of these truths.
> **LEVEL THREE QUESTIONS** will invite you to identify specific action steps you can take to bring to bear what you have learned in both a personal context and in the wider contexts of your family life, church, and community.

IN SUMMARY, EACH STUDY GUIDE CHAPTER INCLUDES THE FOLLOWING MAJOR SECTIONS:

- **INTRODUCTION:** Sets the context for study of the chapter topic.
- **LEARNING OBJECTIVES:** State what you can expect to learn in the chapter.
- **LEVEL ONE QUESTIONS:** Help you identify the key points and biblical arguments presented in the chapter, as well as rebuttals to any counterarguments.
- **LEVEL TWO QUESTIONS:** Aid you in deepening your personal understanding of the biblical truth.
- **LEVEL THREE QUESTIONS:** Invite you to identify action steps you can take to apply what you have learned in both a personal context and in the wider context of your family life, your church, or your community.
- **SUGGESTED ANSWERS TO THE LEVEL ONE QUESTIONS.**

BE TRANSFORMED

If you are a young Christian, relatively new in the faith, you will find yourself "transformed" as you become more established in your faith through your study of *Truths That Transform*. If you are a mature believer, you should gain greater confidence in your ability to discuss these truths with others. The importance of mastering these truths cannot be overstated. Whether you are a young Christian or a mature believer, the great Christian doctrines taught in *Truths That Transform* are "life-changing scriptural truths." Applying them will strengthen your walk and deepen your relationship with Jesus Christ. Dr. Kennedy wrote that "These great old truths of the faith put iron in people's backbones and enable them to stand tall for Christ." May they do so for you!

ENDNOTES:
1 Christian Smith, *Soul Searching: The Religious and Spiritual Lives of American Teenagers* (Oxford, 2005).
2 Chuck Edwards & John Stonestreet, *Why Students Abandon Their Faith: Can we reverse the trend?*
   Truth and Consequences, 2007 – 42 (October)

The Sovereignty of God

INTRODUCTION

After the attack on the World Trade Center on September 11, 2001, people all across America asked, "How could God let that happen?" Then, after the tsunami hit Southeast Asia in December 2005, people around the world asked, "How could God let this happen?"

Perhaps you were among those who asked this question. Perhaps you were among those who tried to answer your friends and family as they asked this question.

This chapter will help you to answer this question for yourself, and it will aid you in giving an answer to those who ask, "Is God really in control?"

LEARNING OBJECTIVES

- To identify the modern, humanist views of God.
- To learn the biblical view of the nature of God.
- To learn what Scripture teaches us concerning God's relation to His creation.
- To learn what Scripture teaches us concerning God's control of human history and individual destiny.
- To respond with head, heart, and will to the scriptural teaching and Christian understanding of God's sovereignty.

LEVEL ONE QUESTIONS

1. The Sovereignty of God is disputed by every man who wants to "usurp the authority of God and be the God of his own life" (See p. 10.) Modern man's view of God, as described by H.G. Wells, is like that of a producer who is frantically rushing around trying to restore order to his stage production, which is rapidly descending into chaos. The argument is that if God were both good and powerful, the world wouldn't be in such a mess. How can we respond to this view of God? (See p. 10.)

_____

_____

THE SOVEREIGNTY OF GOD is His absolute right to do all things according to His own good pleasure.

2. Another argument against God's power and His goodness is based on the assumption that if God were good and powerful, He would not allow Hell to exist as a place of misery and woe. How can we respond to this argument? (See p. 11.)

_____

_____

3. The scriptural view of God is that He is the omnipotent Creator and Ruler of the world. He is all powerful and all holy. List the three specific characteristics of God that are identified in this chapter. How are these characteristics interrelated? (See p. 11.)

_____

_____

_____

_____

4. How would you explain the biblical view of God to a fatalist? (See p. 11.)

_____

_____

_____

FATALISM is the doctrine that all events are predetermined by fate and are therefore unalterable.

5. How can man be *free* if God is indeed sovereign and all His purposes and plans are carried out in creation? (See p. 11.)

_____

_____

_____

6. What is man's great problem? (See p. 11.)

_____

7. What is the biblical response to deism? (See pp. 12-13.)

_____

_____

DEISM is the belief, based solely on reason, in a God who created the universe and then abandoned it, assuming no control over life, exerting no influence on natural phenomena, and giving no supernatural revelation.

8. What are some additional Scriptures which testify that God controls everything, from "the mightiest galaxy to the most infinitesimal atom," even including so-called "fortuitous events"? (See pp. 12-13.)

_____

_____

_____

_____

INVICTUS BY WILLIAM ERNEST HENLEY (1875)

Out of the night that covers me,
    Black as the Pit from pole to pole,
I thank whatever gods may be
    For my unconquerable soul.

In the fell clutch of Circumstance
    I have not winced nor cried aloud.
Under the bludgeonings of Chance
    My head is bloody, but unbowed.

Beyond this place of wrath and tears
    Looms but the Horror of the shade,
And yet the menace of the years
    Finds, and shall find me, unafraid.

It matters not how strait the gate,
    How charged with punishments the scroll,
I am the master of my fate:
    I am the captain of my soul.

9. Does God really control the free acts of men? What scriptural evidence can you provide to support your answer? (See p. 13.)

_____

_____

10. God changed Saul's heart on the way to Damascus. Later, He opened the heart of Lydia so she would attend to Paul's words. What promise do we find in John 6:37 and 6:44 regarding God's work in human hearts? (See p. 14.)

_____

_____

"Though the outward commandments of Christ may be flaunted, ignored, despised, and disobeyed, the secret counsel of Jehovah is coming to pass, and He will make the very wrath of humankind to praise Him" (p. 15).

11. What sobering truth regarding God's sovereignty do we find in Romans 9:16 and 9:18? (See p. 14.)

_____

_____

12. Scripture certainly shows that God is all-powerful and completely sovereign over all the affairs of men and the events in this world. How would you respond to the unbeliever's accusation that if God is all-powerful, He cannot be good, or He would not allow bad things to happen in this world? (See pp. 15–16.)

_____

_____

_____

"God overrules and permits the evil acts of people so that His grace will infallibly be extended to those for whom it is ordained. His justice will inevitably come upon those who reject His Son" (p. 16).

LEVEL TWO QUESTIONS

1. Have you ever doubted whether God is either all good or all powerful?

_____

_____

2. Do you still doubt God's goodness or His ability to help you through difficulties in your life? If so, when do you find it most difficult to trust in God's goodness and His power?

_____

_____

3. Have you ever encountered either of the views that God is not a personal God who is in control of this world (fatalism or deism)? What was your response?

_____

_____

4. If you believe that only God can change the human heart, how does this change what you pray for?

_____

_____

_____

5. How would you explain God's righteousness to a non-Christian? How does our belief in God's righteousness influence our thinking about His power and His goodness? (See pp. 15-16.)

_____

_____

_____

7. Have you ever seen God use for good what another person or persons meant for evil against you, as He did in the life of Joseph? If so, what did that experience teach you?

_____

_____

8. Are you confident that God's mercy has been and will be extended to you? If not, please return to page 16 in _Truths That Transform_ and read the final two paragraphs of this chapter. Truly, Jesus has promised that "the one who comes to Me I will in no wise cast out" (John 6:37), and "he who believes in Me has everlasting life" (John 6:47). What is your response to these promises?

_____

_____

_____

LEVEL THREE QUESTIONS

1. Do you think that you will pray differently now, based on your study of "The Sovereignty of God"?

_____

_____

2. After completing this study, is there anything that you now want to share with a family member, friend, or fellow worker concerning God's sovereignty?

_____

_____

_____

3. What can you express about God's sovereignty with a friend, neighbor, or fellow church member to encourage them?

_____

_____

_____

Father, may we go forth into Your world knowing that You are the sovereign Ruler of every blade of grass. From the atoms in the smallest insect, to the stars that move in their courses, You are the sovereign God. O God, may none of us be guilty of the most grievous sin of rejecting Your grace, mercy, free forgiveness, and gracious gift of life eternal given to those who trust in Christ. For, indeed, every one of us shall one day come to Jesus Christ as Savior in this world, or as Judge in the world which is to come. Amen.

ANSWERS TO LEVEL ONE QUESTIONS

QUESTION 1: The problem is that man is not good or powerful; therefore the world is in the mess it is in.

QUESTION 2: God is good, holy, just, and powerful. Hell is a place where the wicked, sinful, and rebellious are sent. (Also implied here is the truth that the wicked deserve such just punishment due to their sinful and rebellious nature.)

QUESTION 3:
1. The Old Testament presents God as omnipotent. He has all power, and therefore His plan will be worked out.
2. The Old Testament shows the holiness of God. Because He is holy, His plan is morally right.
3. The Old Testament shows the personality of God. God is a Person who is powerful and holy. He is not merely an omnipotent force. He shows us His attributes of love, mercy, wisdom, righteousness, justice, goodness, and truth.

QUESTION 4: Fatalism puts the world's fate into the hands of an impersonal force and rules out all secondary causes. The biblical view is that the world's course is in the hands of God, who is all-righteous, all-wise, and all-merciful. The Bible also affirms that God uses "secondary causes" in carrying out His purposes.

QUESTION 5: Man is free to do "what he pleases," but in his natural state [of sin], he is not free "to do what he ought because he is bound by sin and thus is a bondslave of sin."

QUESTION 6: Man's great problem is the total depravity of his heart and mind.

QUESTION 7: God is in control and is working out His perfect plan for the world. See Isaiah 46:9-11.

QUESTION 8: Proverbs 21:1; Mark 14:30; Proverbs 16:33; I Samuel 14:42; Acts 1:24-26; Job 36:32; I Kings 22:28; Job 14:5.

QUESTION 9: Yes. God controls the free acts of men. See Philippians 2:13 and Exodus 12:35-36.

QUESTION 10: The promise in John 6:37 is that 1) all those whom God the Father has given to the Son will come to the Son, and 2) Those who come will not be cast out, and 3) those whom the Father draws to the Son will be raised up on the last day.

QUESTION 11: God alone can change the human heart, and He will show mercy on those whom He chooses and harden whom He will. He will make the very wrath of humankind to praise Him. "Surely the wrath of man shall praise You; With the remainder of wrath You shall gird Yourself" (Psalm 76:10).

QUESTION 12: 1) God is totally righteous. Man is totally unrighteous. "There is none righteous, no, not one...." (Romans 3:12). 2) Since God is righteous and His judgments are just, and since the heart of every natural man and woman is deceitful and desperately wicked (Jeremiah 17:9-10), God would be absolutely justified in judging all of mankind, even as He did with the Flood in Noah's day. 3) But God is also gracious and has extended His mercy to "a vast multitude whom no one can number." He sent His Son, Jesus Christ, to pay the penalty for the sins of those the Father has given to Him. God's purposes for those He has called will always be done. 4) As the record of Joseph demonstrates in Genesis 37-50, God "overrules and permits the evil acts of people, so that His grace will infallibly be extended to those for whom it is ordained. His justice will inevitably come upon those who reject His Son...."

2

Does Man Have Free Will?

INTRODUCTION

Many people assume that humans are free to make the choices that determine their destinies. Many also assume that democracies should guarantee freedom of choice, even if it means taking the life of an unborn child. However, when questions concerning the nature of our freedom to choose are considered from a spiritual standpoint, we see that there is more involved. Are we really free to choose to do good things, or is there something that restricts us from doing good?

The Apostle Paul struggled with this question and found that, "The good that I will to do, I do not do; but the evil I will not to do, that I practice" (Romans 7:19). As you work through the questions on this chapter, perhaps you will find that some of the answers you previously thought were self-evidently true do not line up with the biblical truths presented. May this study enlighten and encourage you as you consider the question, "Are we really free to do good in our lives?"

LEARNING OBJECTIVES

- To learn the biblical view of the nature of man.
- To learn what Scripture teaches us concerning our ability to please God.
- To learn what Scripture teaches concerning man's ability to do good.
- To respond with head, heart, and will to the scriptural teaching and understanding of human agency.

LEVEL ONE QUESTIONS

1. The question of whether man has a free will is closely connected to the concept of an all-sovereign God. Some claim that the two are mutually exclusive; that is, God cannot be sovereign if man is free to choose, and vice-versa. However, in the opening paragraphs of this chapter, Dr. Kennedy states that the question of whether man has free will is not the proper question. What should our question be? Why? (See p. 17.)

_____

_____

In logic, two mutually exclusive propositions are propositions that cannot both be true.

2. How can we describe the "soul of man," and how does the human will function as a part of our human soul? (See p. 18.)

_____

_____

_____

3. Can you "force" someone to do something "against his will"? Explain your answer. (See pp. 18-19.)

_____

_____

_____

_____

4. What key distinction must be made concerning our ability to choose? (See p. 19.)

_____

_____

_____

5. What is the difference between humanity's "first state" and humanity's "second state?" (See p. 19.)

_____

_____

_____

6. Why is it impossible for the natural man to please God with his good works, no matter how significant they may be? (See p. 20.)

_____

_____

"Some people believe humanity is born in the same condition as was Adam. This is not true. Adam was created in innocence; thereafter, all humans were born in sin. Adam was created free; we are born in bondage to sin" (p. 20).

_____

7. In his book, _The Bondage of the Will_, Luther opposed the views of Erasmus, the religious humanist who wrote on the freedom of the will. What was Luther's view? (See pp. 21-22.)

_____

_____

_____

8. What state is the natural man in? How does this affect what he chooses to do? (See p. 22.)

_____

_____

_____

9. Summarize the biblical teaching about man. (See p. 22.)

_____

_____

_____

_____

LEVEL TWO QUESTIONS

1. Have you ever tried to "force yourself" to do something you really didn't want to do? Or, as a parent or teacher, have you ever tried to force your child or your student to do something he or she didn't want to do? What was the result?

_____

_____

2. As we saw in chapter one, God is sovereign over the affairs of mankind. The events of this world are under His control. In this chapter we have considered the problem of our lack of freedom as human agents to choose to do what we ought. Prior to studying this chapter, what did you believe concerning your ability to make wise or good choices? What do you believe now?

_____

_____

_____

3. How would you respond to the person who claims that he or she does many "good things"?

_____

_____

_____

4. Perhaps one of the most difficult truths taught in this chapter deals with the belief, which is commonly held by many Protestants, that we can somehow choose to leave our sins and come to Jesus Christ on our own accord. Jesus Himself said, "Whosoever commits sin is a slave of sin" (John 8:34). How would you respond to the person who claims that he is free to "choose Christ"? Consider John 8:36 and Romans 9:14-24; pp. 20-21. (Note: In the following chapter this issue will be discussed in greater detail.)

_____

_____

_____

5. This chapter gives a very pointed description of being in bondage to sin. Is there anything in your life which is holding you in bondage? (See p. 21.)

_____

_____

_____

If you identified an emotion, affection, desire, or passion of your sinful nature to which you are still in bondage, you will want to read and study chapter fifteen, "The Holy Spirit," very carefully. One of the works of the Holy Spirit is to cleanse us from our sins. You can begin now by confessing this sin, and then ask God to cleanse you from your sin and fill you with the power of the Holy Spirit.

6. Ultimately, in our natural sinful state, none of us has the ability to do anything except that which is displeasing to God. Have you acknowledged this before God and cried out to the Son of God to set you free? He promises that, "If the Son makes you free, you shall be free indeed!" (John 8:36). If not, you can make the following prayer your personal prayer:

> Lord Jesus, I thank You that You make those who trust in You free. You make them kings and heirs of Your kingdom. You deliver those who come to You from bondage to sin and declare that sin shall no longer have dominion over them. Father, I pray that You will deliver me from the bondage I still live in; a bondage that draws me downward ever deeper into sin. I ask You to set me free from the shackles of sin. Deliver me out of my bondage, darkness, and sin through Christ, the great Emancipator from sin. In His name I pray. Amen.

LEVEL THREE QUESTIONS

1. Among the things we ought to do, and are now able to do through Christ and the power of the Holy Spirit, are: loving God; loving the commandments of God; desiring a holy life; loving purity, holiness, and righteousness. Can you think of actions you can take to increase your love for God and His commandments and your desire for a holy life?

_____

_____

2. How can you encourage your spouse, family members, or other Christians to love purity, holiness, and righteousness?

_____

_____

3. What have you learned through your study of this chapter which you can share with a neighbor or an acquaintance who is struggling to do good things in his or her life and is finding it difficult?

_____

_____

ANSWERS TO LEVEL ONE QUESTIONS

QUESTION 1: We should speak of man as a free agent or a free soul, since the will of man never acts independently from the rest of his faculties. As a human soul, man's will is integral to his entire human being.

QUESTION 2: The soul of man consists of intellect, emotions, and volition. The terms "head," "heart," and "will" are often used for these faculties. When we "choose" to do something or "will" to do it, we are following the direction of our mind and heart, our intellect and emotions. Stated another way, man's will never acts contrary to the direction of his mind and heart.

QUESTION 3: No. Without exception, people always do whatever they please in light of the facts and feelings involved.

QUESTION 4: We are free to choose what we want to do, but the Bible makes it clear that we are not free to do what we ought to do. (See Genesis 6:5; Psalm 14:2-3.) Among the things we ought to do—we ought to love God; repent of our sins; by faith embrace Jesus Christ as our Savior; love the commandments of God; desire a holy life; love purity, holiness, and righteousness.

QUESTION 5: In humanity's "first state" before the fall, Adam and Eve were in a state of innocence and had the ability to do both good and evil. After Adam's fall, in humanity's "second state," we are all born with a fallen nature. Now we have a "natural desire to sin" (Jeremiah 17:9; Romans 3:10-11).

QUESTION 6: The Bible clearly shows that 1) even our "good works" are unacceptable to God, because our motives are wrong, and "They that are in the flesh cannot please God" (Romans 8:8). 2) As long as we are at enmity with God and dead in our sins (Ephesians 2:1, 5), nothing that we do is acceptable to Him as a "good work" (Isaiah 64:6).

QUESTION 7: Luther said that man is bound in sin and controlled by his own passions and desires and cannot cease from these to do good.

QUESTION 8: Natural man is in a state of sin and is a bondslave to sin. Therefore, every choice he makes will always be inclined to sin. The natural man will always choose the wrong thing. He is a servant of his own emotions, affections, desires, and passions. When he looks at Christ, he does not see anything he desires, because his heart and mind give him the wrong message. He does not choose to repent and yield his life to Christ apart from God's grace.

QUESTION 9: Adam, the first man, was in a state of innocence—able to do good and able to sin. Due to Adam's fall, man is now in a state of sin—able only to sin. He is unable to change his moral nature or lift himself up to a state of holiness. When a person is regenerated by the Holy Spirit and has received Jesus into his or her heart as Savior and Lord, that person is in a state of grace. In this state of grace, a person is now able to do good, but is also still able to commit sins. Finally, when those who are in a state of grace come to a state of glory—they are sealed by God and in Heaven are only able to do good.

3

Predestination

INTRODUCTION

Have you measured your spiritual maturity lately? The doctrine of predestination is a "touchstone by which people's characters are revealed," wrote Dr. Kennedy in this chapter. It shows "whether they are truly submissive to Christ and His Word." Furthermore, he wrote, "In studying it, your heart will be revealed to you this hour. You will never be the same. Some of you will hate the thought of predestination; some will love and cherish it. But keep in mind: It is practically impossible to convince the unregenerate mind of this doctrine" (p. 27).

We often hear the first part of Romans 8:28 quoted: "And we know that all things work together for good...." But rarely do we hear the rest of this passage.

> ... To those who love God, to those who are the called according to His purpose. For whom He foreknew, He also predestined to be conformed to the image of His Son, that He might be the firstborn among many brethren. Moreover whom He predestined, these He also called; whom He called He also justified; and whom He justified, these He also glorified.
>
> Romans 8:28-30

As you study this chapter, may you be impressed by God's marvelous grace in predestinating you to be among those whom He has called according to His purpose. Are you rejoicing that you have been "predestined to be conformed to the image of His Son?"

LEARNING OBJECTIVES

- To understand the place of the doctrine of predestination in Church history.
- To learn what Scripture teaches concerning God's predestination of the elect.
- To identify common objections to this doctrine.
- To apprehend the benefits for the Christian of knowing this doctrine.
- To respond with head, heart, and will to the scriptural teaching and understanding of the doctrine of predestination.

LEVEL ONE QUESTIONS

1. As he introduces the doctrine of predestination, Dr. Kennedy points out that it seems to be treated today as something "totally foreign and alien to Christianity." What reasons does he suggest for this reaction? (See p. 26.)

> "As I have talked to thousands of people, I find that most of them are basically convinced that at their heart and in their core, they are basically good" (p. 26).

_____

_____

_____

2. "The unregenerate person, the non-Christian, has an ingrained confidence in his or her fundamentally good nature," wrote Dr. Kennedy on p. 26. But what Scriptures does he cite, which show the opposite is truly the case? What impresses you as you read these Scriptures?

_____

_____

_____

3. Who have been the major figures in history who have set forth the doctrine of predestination? With what historical movement were most of these men associated? Which churches coming out of that movement have also historically adhered to the doctrine of predestination? (See pp. 27-28.)

_____

_____

"The patriots, free-state makers, martyrs, and missionaries of the modern era have been overwhelmingly believers in the doctrine of predestination" (p. 28).

4. Our society is willing to think of God as a "cosmic psychiatrist, a helpful shepherd, a leader, a teacher, anything at all—only not God." Why? (See p. 29.)

_____

_____

5. What is the scriptural view of the doctrine of predestination? What are some of the key Scriptures listed on pages 30-31 that show election, foreordination, and the effectual calling of God's Spirit unto salvation? List them below, then read them in the version you prefer for your personal devotions.

_____

_____

_____

"If we have come to Christ and have been regenerated and redeemed, we may know that we are elect because we would never come otherwise" (p. 30).

6. To understand this doctrine, we must recognize that there are only two things we can receive from God. What are they? (See p. 31.)

_____

_____

7. Charles Spurgeon argued that if we cannot fault God for showing His mercy to those who don't deserve it at all, we cannot argue against God's right to decide, even before the foundation of the world, to show His mercy to someone. How does God's decision to predestinate the elect to Heaven demonstrate His grace? (See p. 32.)

_____

_____

_____

_____

_____

> "And that, my friends, is election, or predestination—that God looked down from all eternity upon a world of sinners and decided to extend mercy to a vast number of people whom no one can number; and that in their appointed time He extended that mercy, not because of anything foreseen in them, but entirely and totally because of what God is—the God of all grace" (p. 32.)

8. The four most common objections to the doctrine of predestination are identified and discussed on pages 32-36. What are these objections? What are Dr. Kennedy's responses to them?

_____

_____

_____

_____

_____

9. Dr. Kennedy states that "the doctrine of election is full of great consolation and there are great practical benefits to holding it and understanding it" (see p. 37). What two benefits does he identify in pages 37–39?

_____

_____

_____

LEVEL TWO QUESTIONS

1. Can you recall hearing the doctrine of predestination preached? If so, how did you respond to that sermon?

_____

_____

2. "The unregenerate person, the non-Christian, has an ingrained confidence in his or her fundamentally good nature," wrote Dr. Kennedy (see p. 26). Can you give an example of a conversation with a family member, friend, or fellow worker in which he or she made the claim that someone was "basically a good person"? How did you respond to that assertion? Would your response be any different now?

_____

_____

_____

3. What view of God have you found to be most prevalent among your family, friends, and co-workers?

_____

_____

4. In Level One, Question 5, you were asked to identify passages in Scripture that deal with predestination and election. Did reading through these passages change your view of your own salvation?

_____

_____

_____

"SALVATION is not by works or human merit, lest anyone should boast. We have nothing to boast about. We also may derive from Scripture this realization that God has created the world for His own glory and not simply for our pleasure. God is glorified because He is a glorious Being.... Thus, in the salvation of the redeemed, the glorious aspects of God's mercy, grace, compassion, long-suffering, kindness, and love are revealed and God is glorified" (p. 34).

5. After reviewing your answers to Level One Questions 6 and 7, how would you describe God's grace and mercy in your own life?

_____

_____

_____

_____

6. Have you ever encountered any of the objections to God's sovereign election that you identified in Level One Question 8? If so, how would you respond to these objections now?

_____

_____

_____

_____

7. Do you see any benefits in holding to and affirming the doctrine of predestination?

_____

_____

_____

_____

8. Are you sure of your election? Read 2 Peter 1:10, John 6:37, and Romans 3:11. If you have come to Jesus and confessed your sins and need of a Savior, be assured that it is because "God, the great and gracious Shepherd, has sought you out and brought you to Himself. The lost sheep does not find the shepherd; the shepherd finds the lost sheep" (p. 39). How does this truth transform your heart and mind?

_____

_____

_____

_____

LEVEL THREE QUESTIONS

1. Is this a doctrine you or someone you know has struggled with in the past? How has your study of this chapter helped you? What means has it provided for you to help others?

_____

_____

_____

_____

2. Has your "heart been revealed to you," through this study, as Dr. Kennedy claimed it would be? Have you changed? If so, what can you share with your spouse or family about the change that has taken place?

_____

_____

_____

_____

3. In what ways will your understanding of predestination affect your prayer life and your witness to those who have not yet received God's gift of eternal life?

_____

_____

_____

_____

ANSWERS TO LEVEL ONE QUESTIONS

QUESTION 1: A. A. Hodge has pointed out that there is a general inattention to this doctrine in the churches and even a prejudice against it. Dr. Kennedy stated that he thought this prejudice comes from the "natural prejudice on the part of people against this doctrine, *as there are to all of the doctrines of grace*" [emphasis added].

QUESTION 2: Matthew 15:19; Jeremiah 17:9-10; Psalm 53:3.

QUESTION 3: a) Augustine, Luther, Calvin, Melanchthon, Zwingli, Knox and Cranmer.
b) The Protestant Reformation. c) Presbyterian and Reformed of Holland, Switzerland and Germany, the Anglicans, the Huguenots, the Covenanters, the Puritans, the Pietists of Germany, the Pilgrims of America.

QUESTION 4: Man wants to be God. This is the essence of sin. We want to be the god of our own lives, and we do not want to give up control or mastery to God or anyone else.

QUESTION 5: There are a group of people known as the elect—those that are chosen of God unto salvation. Matthew 24:22, 24, 31; Luke 10:20; Romans 8:30, 33-34; Ephesians 1:5, 11; I Thessalonians 1:4; 2 Timothy 2:10; Titus 1:1; Revelation 21:27.

QUESTION 6: We can receive God's justice; He is a righteous judge and must be just with everyone. Or we can receive God's mercy and grace, which He is not required to give to anyone.

QUESTION 7: A governor may decide to pardon a criminal, but he is not therefore required to pardon everyone. In the same way, God, from all eternity has decided to extend mercy and forgiveness to individuals who deserve to be punished for their sins and who have done nothing to deserve or earn His forgiveness. Like the governor, God is not required to extend mercy and forgiveness to everyone. But the fact that God has shown His mercy toward anyone of those who are not deserving of it shows His divine grace. (See also I Thessalonians 5:9, "For God did not appoint us to wrath, but to obtain salvation through our Lord Jesus Christ.")

QUESTION 8:

OBJECTION #1: *Why doesn't God save everyone?* Response: 1) God has not revealed His reasons, but they are good and just in His sight (Luke 10:21). 2) We know the reason God has chosen us is not because we are better than anyone else (I Corinthians 1:26-29, 31). 3) God has created the world for His own glory. In the salvation of the redeemed He is glorified, and in the electing of some and the passing by of others, God is glorified.

OBJECTION #2: *Isn't this fatalism?* No. Fatalism allows no place for any human freedom. The Bible teaches that the natural man is free to do what he wants, according to his sinful nature, but he is not free to do what he ought, which is to love God and keep His commandments (Deuteronomy 11:1), because of his sinful nature (Acts 26:18). Because men and women in their sinful state are free to do what they want, they are responsible for their actions and "the liberty and contingency of second causes are maintained, and not destroyed, as they are in fatalism" (p. 35).

OBJECTION #3: *Doesn't this destroy our motivation?* The premise behind this objection is that we are not motivated to do anything if its outcome is certain. But Acts 15:18 says, "Known to God from eternity are all His works." Therefore everything is certain for God. God is omniscient. If He were not, He would not be God. So God knows who will respond to His call of grace, but we are still free to do what we please. "Now this is a mystery we cannot comprehend—how God has ordained all things to work together as people please, and yet God overrules and works everything according to His will" (p. 37). This does not eliminate "the liberty of secondary causes; nor does it mean that people are not free to do what they want" (p. 36).

OBJECTION #4: *If this is true, why should I pray? Why should I witness? Why should I preach?* When we pray to God to convert our friends or relatives, we are, in fact, asking Him to do the very thing that the doctrine of predestination claims He does; i.e., save people by changing their hearts and converting them. If it were not the work of God to do this, we should go and pray to our friend or relative that he would save himself! Furthermore, if God has foreordained someone to be converted, He has also foreordained the means for this conversion: those who pray, those who witness, and those who preach the Gospel so that individuals will be converted. "God never foreordains the ends without also foreordaining means" (p. 37).

QUESTION 9:

BENEFIT #1: This doctrine shows that salvation is all of grace from beginning to end. It is all of God. He is the One who seeks us and draws us unto Himself.

BENEFIT #2: This doctrine gives great security and courage to those who believe it. Those who know that God sovereignly controls every atom of this universe are filled with good courage and confidence.

4

Effectual Calling

INTRODUCTION

The previous three chapters deal with some profound truths; truths that truly transform our understanding of God and His relationship to His creation. God's sovereignty, the bondage of man's will to sin, and God's predestination of the elect are not easy doctrines to understand. Some struggle to accept them. They are, as we saw in the last chapter, a kind of measure of our spiritual maturity. Each one shows our weakness and inability to do anything to establish ourselves in a right relationship with God—and thereby challenges our pride.

The subject of this chapter is the way in which our redemption, which has been procured by Christ and ordained by God, is to be applied. The doctrine that expresses this is called *effectual calling*. It shows how God carries out His plan to draw the elect to Himself. For as Romans 8:30 states, "whom He did predestinate, them He also called."

If you or someone you know is asking, "Am I called by God?" you will find your answer in studying this chapter on *effectual calling*.

LEARNING OBJECTIVES

- To learn the doctrine of *effectual calling.*
- To learn what Scripture teaches concerning the two kinds of calling.
- To recognize the other terms used in referring to this doctrine.
- To distinguish between the Calvinist and the Arminian views of God's calling and to understand the two basic problems with the latter view.
- To recognize the marvel of God's grace contained in His call.
- To respond with head, heart, and will to the scriptural teaching and understanding of God's call.

LEVEL ONE QUESTIONS

1. The Bible speaks of two kinds of calling; there is a calling that is effectual and a calling that is not. Which key verse of Scripture is identified on page 42 in relation to effectual calling?

_____

_____

_____

EFFECTUAL: That which works, is successful, and succeeds in doing what the author intends.

2. There is an important difference between the effectual call and the mere outward call. When the outward call, which comes through preaching of the Word, is accompanied by the work of the Holy Spirit, that outward call becomes effectual. Thus the Spirit of God "effectually woos and draws us to Christ so we come freely, being made willing by His grace." Why, according to Scripture, must the work of the Holy Spirit accompany the outward calling of the Word in order for us to be "effectually called"? (See pp. 42-43.)

_____

_____

_____

4. Chapter X of the Westminster Confession states the doctrine of effectual calling. How does the Confession describe the "wooing" of the Holy Spirit in drawing us to Jesus Christ? (See p. 44.)

_____

_____

5. Identify the agent, the instrument, and the objects of effectual calling. (See p. 44.)

"But we are bound to give thanks to God always for you, brethren beloved by the Lord, because God from the beginning chose you for salvation through sanctification by the Spirit and belief in the truth, to which He called you by our gospel, for the obtaining of the glory of our Lord Jesus Christ" (2 Thessalonians 2:13-14).

6. There are two theological systems within Protestantism that have attempted to answer the question, "Why don't all who hear the Gospel of Jesus Christ embrace Him as their Savior?" These two systems are Arminianism and Calvinism. Which system answers this question by focusing on man, and which answers it by looking to God and His sovereign choice? What is one of the Scriptures that Calvinists use in support of their view? (See p. 45.)

_____

_____

_____

7. Dr. Kennedy identifies two basic problems with the Arminian view. Summarize these two problems. (See pp. 46–47.)

_____

_____

_____

"Do we have a God who is desperately trying to save everybody and is equally failing; or do we have a God who has set His purpose and fixed His heart upon His own people, His elect, whom He has chosen before the foundation of the world? The sovereign Lord God of Heaven and earth is unfailingly bringing every one of them into glory!" (pp. 47-48).

8. If it were not for God's grace, no one would be saved! It is man's own sinful heart that leads him to perdition. What are the two things that are necessary for man to be reborn? (See p. 48.)

_____

_____

_____

"The Holy Spirit takes away the dead sinners' darkened minds, illumines their understanding, unstops their ears, takes away their hearts of stone, gives them hearts of flesh, and renews their dead wills. After hearing the invitation, sinners say, "I will come to Thee, O Christ." Afterward they know it was Christ who brought them to Himself" (p. 49).

LEVEL TWO QUESTIONS

1. How did you previously view the work of the Holy Spirit in bringing sinners to salvation in Jesus Christ? Has this study deepened your understanding of His work?

_____

_____

_____

_____

2. In Reformed churches, the term irresistible grace is often used rather than the term effectual calling. Have you ever tried to "resist" God's grace in your life? Can you see, in looking back, how, in spite of your resistance, He "wooed" and won you to Him?

The Reformed churches often refer to the Canons of Dordt rather than the Westminster Confession of Faith as a statement reflecting the Calvinist understanding of the nature of divine grace and predestination as it relates to salvation. The Synod of Dordt was convened in 1618 by the Dutch Reformed Church in order to settle the controversy in the Dutch churches initiated by the rise of Arminianism.

_____

_____

_____

_____

3. After studying this chapter, how would you respond to the person who says, "If God is offering all people the choice of eternal life, then it is up to each person to decide whether to choose it or not." (See pp. 46-47.)

_____

_____

_____

"Man is always free to do what he wants; that is why he is responsible for everything he does. But he doesn't have the power to do what he ought. He ought to love God ... but he cannot change his character any more than the Ethiopian can change his skin or the leopard his spots" (p. 46).

4. Can you state for sure that you are one of God's elect? If you have come to Christ, you can know that you are, because you never would have come otherwise! The promise is, "Whosoever shall call upon the name of the Lord shall be saved" (Acts 2:21). Looking back, we can see that it was the Spirit of God who drew us to Himself.

> I sought the Lord, and afterward I knew
> He moved my soul to seek Him, seeking me;

It was not I that found, O Savior true,
No, I was found, was found of thee.

Author Unknown

Describe how God found you.

_____

_____

_____

_____

5. What can you say about God's effectual calling that is expressed in Isaiah 55:11?

So shall My word be that goes forth from My mouth;
It shall not return to Me void,
But it shall accomplish what I please,
And it shall prosper in the thing for which I sent it.

_____

_____

_____

LEVEL THREE QUESTIONS

1. If we want others to know what Christ can do for them, we can tell them what Christ has done for us. How can you share with a family member, friend, or fellow worker how God used His Word and His Spirit to draw you to Himself?

_____

_____

_____

2. What have you learned through your study of this chapter that you can share with someone who is wondering if they are called by God?

_____

_____

_____

_____

_____

ANSWERS TO LEVEL ONE QUESTIONS

QUESTION 1: Isaiah 55:11 "[My word] shall not return to Me void. But it shall accomplish what I please, and it shall prosper in the thing for which I sent it."

QUESTION 2: When the call to come to Jesus in order to receive Him is preached or declared, John 6:37 tells us that God will refuse no one who comes in response to that call. But man is so bound by sin and blinded by his iniquity, he has no desire to respond and Romans 3:11 shows "there is none that seeks after God." Furthermore, God declares that when we seek after Him, we shall find Him (Jeremiah 29:13), yet it is clear that no one in his or her natural state of sin seeks after God because "the natural man receives not the things of the Spirit of God" (1 Corinthians 2:14). So it is the work of the Holy Spirit to draw us to God through an inward call. This is seen in Romans 8:30. All who are elect (see chapter three) will come to Him (John 6:37). See also Psalm 110:3; Jonah 2:9; Romans 9:16; Titus 3:4-6.

QUESTION 3: Irresistible Grace and Efficacious Grace.

QUESTION 4: We are altogether passive until, "being quickened and renewed" by the Holy Spirit, we are thereby enabled to answer the outward call and to embrace the grace offered and conveyed in it.

QUESTION 5: The agent is the Holy Spirit. The instrument is the Word of God. The objects of effectual calling are unregenerate sinners—specifically those of God's elect.

QUESTION 6: The Arminian focuses on man. The Calvinist focuses on God and refers to
I Corinthians 4:7, "For who makes you differ from another? And what do you have that
you did not receive? Now if you did indeed receive it, why do you boast as if you had not
received it?"

QUESTION 7: *The two problems are found in 1) the nature of man and 2) the nature of God.*
1) Because of the Fall, man is spiritually dead, and nothing but the power of God can
deliver him from that state. He does not have any power in himself to become holy
before God, nor does he even want to do so. (See Psalm 51:5; Romans 3:11.) "So the first
problem with the Arminian view is that man is not free to do what he ought to do" (p. 46).
2) The Arminian view of God is also a problem because, according to that view, God is
"trying desperately to save everybody in the world, but it is up to us to determine
whether we are going to let Him" (p. 46). This view places the will of man above the will
of God and denies His sovereignty over all things, including the spirit, the will, and
the heart of man (Romans 9:19; Ephesians 1:9).

QUESTION 8: God's Spirit and God's Word. It is necessary to have the outward calling of the
Word and the inward calling of the Holy Spirit, "who takes the gospel of Jesus Christ and makes
it a life-creating force that quickens dead sinners from death in sin and brings them to life
in Christ" (p. 49).

5

The Incomparable Christ

INTRODUCTION

Have you ever encountered someone who claimed, "There are many ways to Heaven"?
Or perhaps you are not so sure yourself that Jesus is the only way to the Father, as He claimed in John 14:6, when He said, "I am the way, the truth, and the life. No one comes to the Father except through Me."

Missionaries to India must show that Jesus Christ is "the incomparable Christ" to Hindus, who otherwise assume they can set Him alongside their thousand gods, rather than acknowledge that He alone is Savior and Lord. How often do we fail to recognize the glorious virtues of our incomparable Christ, or even stand by as others defame His name? If Jesus is not unlike any other, then there would be no reason for every knee to bow at His name and for every tongue to confess that Jesus Christ is Lord, to the glory of God the Father, as the Apostle Paul states in Philippians 2:10-11.

As you study this chapter, consider these questions: Is there anyone who compares to Christ? Is He truly incomparable?

LEARNING OBJECTIVES

- To identify the reasons we should contrast Jesus Christ with the founders of all other religions.
- To learn the basic characteristics of these religions.
- To learn the three great differences between Christ and the founders of these religions.
- To respond with head, heart, and will to the scriptural teaching of the uniqueness of Christ.

LEVEL ONE QUESTIONS

1. What are three reasons Dr. Kennedy identified for comparing Jesus Christ with the founders of the world's other major religions? (See p. 52.)

_____

_____

_____

_____

"The fact that you are a member of a Christian church does not necessarily mean you are a Christian; but if you are truly a Christian, I hope that you will see more clearly the tremendous privilege and blessing you have received" (p. 52).

2. Dr. Kennedy has pointed out that evolutionists claim the world's religions have "evolved" from polytheistic animism to the monotheistic religions of today. But archeology has confirmed that monotheism was primary among the world's cultures. Today animism is practiced in parts of Africa, South America, and throughout Asia. There are even animists in the United States and Canada. The Bible tells us that people originally knew God, but they became vain in their imaginations and their foolish hearts were darkened so that

they served the creature rather than the Creator (Romans 1:20-23). Describe how animism fits the description of Romans 1. (See pp. 53-54.)

_____

_____

_____

_____

ANIMISM is the belief in the existence of individual spirits that inhabit natural objects and phenomena.

3. Hinduism, the world's third largest religion, has close to one billion people. The majority of Hindus live in India and Nepal, but other countries with large Hindu populations include Bangladesh, Sri Lanka, Pakistan, Indonesia, Malaysia, Singapore, Mauritius, Fiji, Suriname, Guyana, and Trinidad and Tobago. How did Hinduism originate? What is the most basic element of this religion? What is the only thing that the Hindu ultimately has to look forward to? (See pp. 54-55.)

_____

_____

_____

_____

_____

_____

_____

_____

"Hindus hope through understanding that the world does not really exist and that all is God and by meditating upon the great existing God, they can finally, through a number of reincarnations, achieve nirvana. They feel that this may take thousands of reincarnations of continual suffering. . . . The great thing they are looking for is the extinction of life, nirvana, where one finally becomes extinct and ceases to be reborn into further cycles of life, where the individual soul drops back into the ocean and ceases to have any individual consciousness" (p. 55).

4. Buddhism is practiced primarily in the countries of Asia, but it has been carried to the West by travelers who went there seeking "enlightenment." It may have 500 million adherents throughout the world. What is the origin of Buddhism? What is the major problem that both Buddhism and Hinduism are seeking to answer? How does Buddhism's answer differ from that of Hinduism? (See pp. 55-56.)

"A Buddhist does not admit the existence of God. Buddha was an atheist. He denied any God or gods. He denied prayer. He denied all the priests and Brahmans" (p. 56).

_____

_____

_____

_____

5. Confucianism, like Buddhism, is more of an ethical and philosophical system than a religion. Confucianism is strongest in China (including Hong Kong and Macau), Taiwan, Japan, Korea, Singapore, and Vietnam as well in those areas that have been settled by Chinese. What are some of the basic beliefs of Confucianism? What hope does it offer? (See pp. 56-57.)

_____

_____

_____

_____

6. The world's second largest religion is Islam. It is practiced throughout the Middle East and parts of Asia and Africa. Muslims believe that God revealed the Koran to Muhammad, who

lived six centuries after Christ. They regard Muhammad as God's final prophet. They do not see him as the founder of a new religion, but as the restorer of the original monotheistic faith of Abraham, Moses, and other prophets. Jesus is considered by Muslims to be only a prophet and He is secondary to Muhammad. Today there are five major types of Islam with 21 subdivisions within them. What hope does Islam offer? What means have its followers used to spread their religion both in the past and today? (See p. 57.)

_____

_____

_____

_____

_____

"Do not divide your religion into sects, each exulting in its own doctrines" (The Koran, Surah 30:30).

7. How does Dr. Kennedy describe Judaism? (See p. 57.)

_____

_____

_____

_____

_____

_____

8. Dr. Kennedy has identified three great differences between Christ and the founders of all other religions. The first is that Jesus Christ is an incarnate deity. He is God Himself come into this world. His divinity was confirmed by a life that is absolutely unique. What are some of the ways Jesus Christ's life on earth was unique? (See pp. 58–60.)

_____

_____

_____

_____

_____

9. What are the other two major differences between Jesus Christ and the founders of the other religions? (See pp. 60–61.)

_____

_____

_____

LEVEL TWO QUESTIONS

1. How has your study of this chapter enabled you to see more clearly who Jesus Christ is?

_____

_____

_____

2. What do you appreciate now about Christianity that you did not appreciate before?

_____

_____

_____

_____

3. What have you learned about the other religions of the world that has increased your compassion, pity, and love for those who adhere to these religions?

_____

_____

_____

_____

4. Read again the story on page 60-61 of the man in the pit. Would you consider sharing this story with the follower of another religion in order to show Christ's uniqueness? What else would you want to tell that person in order to explain His uniqueness?

_____

_____

_____

_____

TRUTHS THAT TRANSFORM STUDY GUIDE

5. What have you found to be the most overlooked aspect of the person and work of Christ among your family members, friends, or fellow workers—even among those who claim to be Christians?

_____

_____

_____

_____

6. Have you encountered anyone who has denied Christ's divinity? What would you want to share with that person now concerning the incomparable Christ?

_____

_____

_____

_____

7. Although Christianity is the world's largest religion, there are billions who live "without Christ . . . having no hope and without God in the world" (Ephesians 2:12). There will come a day when "every tongue will confess that Jesus Christ is Lord, to the glory of God the Father" (Philippians 2:11 NASB), whether they have served Him in this life or not. Has your study of this chapter motivated you to a greater effort to reach those who do not know Christ in order to share the Good News of salvation through Him?

_____

_____

_____

_____

LEVEL THREE QUESTIONS

1. In what ways will the deepened understanding you have gained of the uniqueness of Christ affect your relationship with Him?

_____

_____

_____

_____

_____

2. How has our culture and society demeaned the name of Christ and denied His uniqueness?

_____

_____

_____

_____

_____

3. How do you plan to share the incomparable Christ with members of your family, friends, or fellow workers who do not know Him as their Savior and Lord?

_____

_____

_____

_____

4. After considering your plan, ask God's help and pray the following prayer:

> O God, grant us a compassion and pity on those who live in darkness
> and fear, without hope in this life or for the life to come. We pray
> that You will grant us a new zeal to take the love of Jesus Christ, and
> that hope of everlasting bliss that He alone can give, to all of the world.
> We pray for those who have never met Him. May they come to know
> Him personally. May they invite Him into their hearts and lives.
> We ask this in that blessed name, which is above every name, even
> Jesus Christ the Lord. Amen.

ANSWERS TO LEVEL ONE QUESTIONS

QUESTION 1: First, so that we might see more clearly who Jesus Christ is. Second, so we can gain a greater appreciation of what it is that Christians have received in Christ. Third, we need to understand what our attitude toward those who follow other religions should be—pity, compassion, and love.

QUESTION 2: Animists worship parts of creation, believing that inanimate objects and even animals have living spirits and therefore possess powers that are able to control humans. Animism is a religion of dread and fear and, indeed, has "exchanged the glory of the incorruptible God for . . . birds and four-footed animals and creeping things" (Romans 1:23).

QUESTION 3: Hinduism originated in India around 1500 B.C. when the Aryans from the Iranian plateau conquered the aboriginal people of India and set up a caste system based on color as a system of segregation. Even today, this is the most basic element of this religion. The only thing that the Hindu ultimately has to look forward to is nirvana, which comes about when the individual soul finally ceases to be reincarnated into further cycles of life and no longer has any individual consciousness. He is, in the end, working for nothing.

QUESTION 4: Both Buddhism and Hinduism are seeking to answer the problem of pain and suffering. The Buddhist differs from the Hindu in answering this problem by saying that the reason for suffering is not ignorance, as the Hindu claims, but rather our desires and emotions. People suffer because they desire things they cannot have. According to the Buddhist, the key to easing human suffering is to eliminate all desire.

QUESTION 5: Confucianism teaches filial piety. The duties and obligations of subjects to their emperors, wives to their husbands, children to their parents, and youngsters to elders are emphasized. Confucius was an agnostic and did not offer any hope after this life. He asked, "How can we know about death when we do not even know about life?"

QUESTION 6: Islam offers no certainty for the hope of entering paradise. Adherents will only find out at the time of their death if they will be allowed to enter the sensual paradise described in the Koran. Islam has been spread by means of conquest and coercion, both in the past and even today. Those who will not accept Islam often suffer death.

QUESTION 7: "Judaism is simply the biblical religion with its head cut off—truncated without Christ—the heart of which is a sacrificial system which says that without the shedding of blood there is no remission of sins. All of the sacrificial system was ended with the destruction of Jerusalem, so now Judaism has a vacuum at its core" (p. 56).

QUESTION 8: Some of the ways Jesus Christ's life on earth was unique include the following: 1) He never withdrew or modified any statement He ever made; 2) He never apologized for anything He said because He was never wrong; 3) He never sought advice from anyone because, as God, He knew everything; 4) He never justified His behavior; 5) He never asked for prayer for Himself, but told His disciples to pray for themselves; 6) He did not have any weak points; 7) He was altogether lovely in every way; 8) He mixed truth with gentleness in a perfect measure.

QUESTION 9: The other two major differences between Jesus Christ and the founders of the other religions are:
1) Jesus came not just as a teacher—He came to die for our sins.
2) Jesus rose from the dead after He was in the grave for three days.
By His life, death, and resurrection, He has declared that He is God Himself.

6

Repentance

INTRODUCTION

Have you ever considered the truth Dr. Kennedy pointed out in the opening of this chapter, "Repentance itself will not save you; yet you cannot be saved without it"? We want people to repent of their horrible acts or evil things they have said, thought, or done—for example Jeffrey Dahmer or Osama bin Laden. However, even if a person repents and confesses his crimes, even if he turns from his terrible deeds and tries to do good, he still cannot gain entry into Heaven.

Why? Why is repentance necessary for us to gain entry into Heaven, yet not sufficient to open Heaven's doors for us when we die? As you study this chapter, consider how a biblical understanding of repentance transforms your relationship with God. Consider also how this enables you to share with others why repentance is necessary, but not sufficient to open Heaven's door.

LEARNING OBJECTIVES

- To learn the biblical teaching concerning repentance.
- To learn what Scripture teaches concerning the relationship between faith and repentance.
- To learn that repentance is a gift.
- To respond with head, heart, and will to the scriptural teaching and understanding of repentance.

LEVEL ONE QUESTIONS

1. The Bible teaches the importance of repentance in both the Old and New Testaments. Who are some of those who preached repentance? (See p. 64.)

_____

_____

2. What did Jesus say about repentance, as recorded in Luke? (See p. 64.)

_____

_____

_____

3. On the day of Pentecost, what was the first thing Peter told the people when they asked what they should do to be saved? (See p. 64.)

_____

_____

_____

4. In spite of the importance of this basic doctrine, many churches fail to preach the need for repentance. List the two reasons the Reformed theologian R. B. Kuiper gave for this fact. (See p. 65.)

_____

_____

_____

"People have lost their vision of the holy God. They do not lift up their eyes, because if they once saw God, they would abhor themselves and repent in dust and ashes." — R. B. Kuiper

5. How are repentance and faith related in Scripture? (See p. 65.)

_____

_____

_____

6. How are the three parts of the human soul involved in true faith and repentance? (See pp. 65-66.)

_____

_____

_____

7. Explain why repentance must be a gift of God's grace. (See p. 66.)

_____

_____

_____

_____

"People may be moved to tears by a sermon and even decide they're going to do something about their sin. But if their decision is not based on a proper understanding of the Gospel, they will trust in their own efforts to do better and soon be back wallowing in the mud of sin, despair, and frustration" (p. 66).

LEVEL TWO QUESTIONS

1. Do you know someone who continually says he or she is sorry for hurting you in some way, but then continues to do the same thing? Have you ever done this in repenting of something you have done?

_____

_____

2. At the beginning of this chapter, Dr. Kennedy stated that even a "change of heart" is sufficient to gain forgiveness of our sins. Because God is just, He also requires that a penalty must be paid for our sins. Have you found yourself, or perhaps someone you know, thinking that just feeling sorrow for the wrongs one commits is sufficient to receive God's forgiveness? What have you learned in this chapter that demonstrates why this is not enough ?

_____

_____

_____

_____

_____

> "It is only as we see the awfulness of our own sins and truly desire in our hearts to turn from them and embrace the Savior that God accepts our repentance. This repentance is not something we can do of ourselves; it is not merely an effort to turn over a new leaf and try to do better" (p. 66).

_____

3. Has your understanding of the relationship between faith and repentance changed through studying this chapter?

_____

_____

_____

4. Can you think of examples that support the claim made by R. B. Kuiper that people have lost sight of the real meaning of sin and lost their vision of the holy God?

_____

_____

_____

_____

5. The three parts of the human soul—the intellect, the heart, and the will—must all be involved in true repentance. Do you find it more difficult to grasp the heinousness of your sin intellectually or to have true contrition for your sin? What do you think you can do to achieve both?

_____

_____

_____

_____

_____

6. When Christ returns to this earth as King of Kings and Lord of Lords, all mankind will stand before the throne of God to be judged according to our works, as described in Revelation 20:12-15. The time to repent and ask for God's forgiveness through the atoning work of Christ will have passed. Only those whose names are already written in the Lamb's Book of Life will enter into eternal life. Will your name be found there? Have you repented of your sins with a broken and contrite heart and turned to Christ in faith, embracing Him as your Lord and Savior?

> Oh God, deliver us from being deceived. Grant unto us a new sense of the heinousness of our sins and the holiness of God. May we turn from them all to walk in the ways of new obedience. Cause us to mourn for our sins and turn unto You, O Lord Jesus Christ, for You have been lifted up on the Cross that we might be saved if we will repent and believe. Amen

LEVEL THREE QUESTIONS

1. How can you walk in true repentance and faith in Jesus?

_____

_____

_____

_____

2. How can you encourage your spouse or family members or other Christians to do the same?

_____

_____

_____

_____

3. What have you learned through your study of this chapter that you plan to share with a neighbor or an acquaintance who has not professed faith in Jesus and who does not see the need for repentance for sin and faith in Christ?

_____

_____

_____

_____

_____

ANSWERS TO LEVEL ONE QUESTIONS

QUESTION 1: Some of those who preached repentance were Noah, Nahum, and the other prophets, John the Baptist and Jesus.

QUESTION 2: Luke records that Jesus said, "Unless you repent you will all likewise perish" (Luke 13:3) and "Thus it is written, and thus it was necessary for the Christ to suffer and to rise from the dead the third day, and that repentance and remission of sins should be preached in His name to all nations, beginning at Jerusalem" (Luke 24:46-47).

QUESTION 3: At Pentecost, the first thing Peter told the people when they asked what they should do to be saved was that they should "Repent!" (Acts 2:38).

QUESTION 4: The two reasons the Reformed theologian R. B. Kuiper gave for the fact that many churches do not preach repentance are:
     1) People have lost sight of the true meaning of sin.
     2) People have lost a vision of the holiness of God.

QUESTION 5: Repentance and faith are inseparable in Scripture. There can be no genuine repentance without faith, and there is no genuine faith without repentance. False faith or mere intellectual assent will not bring forth true repentance. Repentance without saving faith only causes one to rely on one's own good works.

QUESTION 6: The three parts of the human soul must all be involved in true faith and repentance. The intellect must grasp the truth that: a) sin must be punished by God, b) there is only one divine remedy for sin, and c) it is only through Christ's death and resurrection that we have hope of eternal life. In addition to an intellectual comprehension of these truths, we must come to God with a contrite heart that acknowledges our sins. We must willfully renounce our sins as we repent of them and turn toward Christ in faith, trusting in His ability to save us from our sins.

QUESTION 7: Repentance must be a gift of God's grace, because we are incapable of turning from our sins and trusting in Jesus for forgiveness apart from the work of the Holy Spirit. (See Chapter Four, "Effectual Calling.") As 2 Timothy 2:24-25 states, "And a servant of the Lord must not quarrel but be gentle to all, able to teach, patient, in humility correcting those who are in opposition, *if God perhaps will grant them repentance*, [emphasis added] so that they may know the truth."

7

Faith

INTRODUCTION

"Faith," as Dr. Kennedy has said, "is the key that unlocks the door to Heaven." We all desire to have such a key. But we may be kidding ourselves. We may believe that we have "true faith" when, in reality, our faith is not resting on the proper object. Or we may have a "faith" that does not originate from the proper source.

In this chapter we will see the true nature of faith, its proper object, and its true origin. May your study of this chapter give you the assurance that your faith will truly unlock the door of Heaven for you.

"For by grace you have been saved through faith, and that not of yourselves; it is the gift of God, not of works, lest anyone should boast" (Ephesians 2:8-9).

LEARNING OBJECTIVES

- To learn the nature of true faith.
- To learn what Scripture teaches concerning the true object of faith.
- To learn the acts of saving faith.
- To learn what Scripture teaches concerning the true origin of faith.
- To respond with head, heart, and will to the scriptural teaching and understanding of saving faith.

LEVEL ONE QUESTIONS

1. On pages 70-71, a number of examples are provided for what Dr. Kennedy calls "indolent assent." How can people claim they have "faith," he asks, if "professing to believe, they act throughout the week in point-blank opposition to what they have heard on Sunday?" What evidence should we present to demonstrate that we have indeed believed a statement to be true?

_____

_____

_____

_____

"If a person believes something concerning a matter which involves action, he will inevitably do that which his belief demands" (p. 72).

2. How can you identify a person who does not have faith? (See p. 72.)

_____

_____

_____

3. Define "true faith." (See p. 72.)

_____

_____

4. The meaning of faith, as Dr. Kennedy explains, is found in our accepting or seeing that something is true. How does our will enter into our acceptance of something as true? (See p. 73.)

_____

_____

_____

_____

5. How does our personal disposition or temperament affect our ability to carry out or act upon the things that we believe? (See p. 73.)

_____

_____

_____

"If you believed, you would be transformed by that belief. 'If any man be in Christ, he is a new creature [a new creation]' (2 Corinthians 5:17)" (p. 73).

6. The Westminster Confession of Faith, Chapter XIV, states, "By this faith, a Christian believeth to be true whatsoever is revealed in the Word, for the authority of God Himself speaking therein." What should be the object of our faith—in the broadest sense? (See p. 74.)

_____

_____

_____

_____

7. What are the principle acts of saving faith? (See p. 74.)

_____

_____

_____

8. When we receive and rest upon Christ, He comes to us in all His grace and glory as our High Priest, our Sacrifice, our Surety. He has offered Himself in our stead and promises us eternal life. We can accept Him on the basis of the promises of God's Word. Identify some of those promises. (See p. 74.)

_____

_____

_____

_____

_____

> "When we come to believe His Word and trust in Him, we are reconciled to God, our sins are forgiven, and we are made heirs of eternal life, adopted into His family, and become the children of God. When we believe that we are saved, our lives are invariably transformed" (pp. 74-75).

9. Why do people not believe? What is the origin of saving faith? (See p. 75.)

_____

_____

_____

_____

_____

_____

LEVEL TWO QUESTIONS

1. In what areas of your life have you claimed to "believe" something to be true, but you have not followed through with actions that would line up with that belief?

_____

_____

_____

2. Can you identify a biblical doctrine or truth that you have had or even now have difficulty believing? Is it because you are still wondering if it is true?

_____

_____

_____

_____

3. Now that you have studied this chapter, how would you respond to the person who claims that he or she "has faith," but they are not showing any actions that would give evidence of that faith? What Scripture could you show them? (See p. 72.)

_____

_____

_____

_____

4. Have you or one of your family members ever said, "I just don't feel like doing that" in a situation where God's Word made it clear what should be done? What does that statement tell you about the nature of your faith or theirs in that instance?

_____

_____

_____

"But I say to you, look unto Him who has died in your place and paid your penalty. Look unto Him whose hands are extended unto you and offering you life eternal. There is life for a look at the Crucified One. Look—and believe!" (p. 75).

5. Have you accepted, received, and rested in Christ alone for justification, sanctification, and eternal life? How have those acts of saving faith changed you?

_____

_____

_____

_____

6. As you look back at the events in your life that led to the point when you received Christ in faith, can you see how the Spirit of God was at work in your heart?

_____

_____

_____

_____

LEVEL THREE QUESTIONS

1. Are there any transforming truths of God's Word that you believe now that you did not believe as a young Christian? Do you know a new or young Christian you can encourage by sharing your testimony in this area?

_____

_____

_____

_____

2. What have you learned in the study of this chapter that you can share with a family member, friend, or fellow worker who is struggling with doubts about his or her faith?

_____

_____

_____

_____

3. What transforming truth have you learned from this chapter that you now accept as true and will therefore act upon?

_____

_____

_____

_____

4. If there is someone you desire to see receive, accept, and rest in Christ, you can pray this prayer for that person.

> Father, I pray that Your Spirit may graciously and sovereignly open the eyes of _____ that he/she may see the light of Your glory shining in the face of Jesus Christ. May _____ take hold of Him by faith and be transformed by His Love. In His lovely name. Amen.

ANSWERS TO LEVEL ONE QUESTIONS

QUESTION 1: The evidence that we have, indeed, believed a statement to be true should be seen in our action following our belief.

QUESTION 2: "People who are not moved to a correspondent action or volition by what they hear are people without faith" (p. 72).

QUESTION 3: "True faith is a divine work of God in our hearts that makes us new in all our faculties." Such faith is busy and active. "Faith that does not produce a transformed life is a vain, empty illusion and is no real faith at all" (p. 72).

QUESTION 4: It does not. I may accept something as true either willingly or unwillingly. But once I accept it as true, I believe it; I have faith in it.

QUESTION 5: Disposition or temperament has nothing to do with our acting on the things we say we believe. If we say we believe, we will act on our belief. We would be transformed by that belief.

QUESTION 6: In the broadest sense, the object of our faith should be whatever is revealed in the Word of God.

QUESTION 7: The principal acts of saving faith are "accepting, receiving, and resting upon Christ alone for justification, sanctification, and eternal life, by virtue of the covenant of grace" (Westminster Confession of Faith, Chapter XIV, Article 2).

QUESTION 8: Some of the promises in God's Word that we can rest on include:
    1) John 3:16, "For God so loved the world that He gave His only begotten Son, that whoever believes in Him should not perish but have everlasting life."

2) John 6:37, "All that the Father gives Me will come to Me, and the one who comes to Me I will by no means cast out."

3) John 3:18, "He who believes in Him is not condemned; but he who does not believe is condemned already, because he has not believed in the name of the only begotten Son of God."

QUESTION 9: People do not believe because: 1) they have some false or distorted notion of the Word of God that does not allow them to understand or believe what it says, and/or 2) they have been blinded by Satan, who is always seeking to delude our minds, even as he did in Jesus' day (Mark 8:18).

The origin of true faith is through the work of the Spirit of God in our hearts. "…[U]nless one is born again, he cannot see the kingdom of God" (John 3:3). (See also Chapter Four, "Effectual Calling.")

8

Justification

INTRODUCTION

Do you celebrate Reformation Day, October 31? On this day in 1517, Martin Luther posted his *95 Theses* on the doors of the Castle Church in Wittenberg, Germany. Within two weeks this document had spread throughout Germany; within two months throughout Europe.

Why such interest in a long Latin document posted on a church door? Luther had called for debate on the doctrine and practice of indulgences. The Roman Catholic Church of his day sold indulgences. According to the Roman Catholic doctrine, an indulgence, based on the accumulated good deeds of the saints, could provide the remission of punishment for a sin already committed. Luther saw that the selling of indulgences was deluding the people. They were trying to buy remission of sins rather than trusting in Christ to be justified from their sins. In his commentary on Galatians, Luther later wrote, "As I often emphasize, the doctrine of justification must be diligently observed. In it are involved all other articles of our faith, and so long as justification is properly taught, it will be well with all other doctrines also."[1]

Do you understand the doctrine of justification? After studying this chapter, perhaps you will celebrate October 31 as Reformation Day: a day for recognizing the heritage we have received from Reformers such as Martin Luther—a day for celebrating our justification by faith in Jesus Christ.

LEARNING OBJECTIVES

- To understand and learn the doctrine of justification.
- To learn what Scripture teaches us concerning the reality of our sin and guilt and God's remedy for it.
- To learn what Scripture teaches concerning the work of Christ.
- To learn the nature of justification by faith.
- To respond with head, heart, and will to the scriptural teaching and understanding of justification.

LEVEL ONE QUESTIONS

1. The doctrine of justification is the Gospel of our Lord Jesus Christ, for it answers our greatest need; i.e., the need to know how we can stand in the presence of God and be rightly related to Him. Before we can approach God, what two realities about your human condition must we accept? (See pp. 78-80.)

_____

_____

_____

> "If we are to appreciate that which is central in the Gospel, if the jubilee trumpet is to find its echo again in our hearts, our thinking must be revolutionized by the realism of the wrath of God, of the reality and gravity of our guilt, and of the divine condemnation upon it" (p. 79).

2. God hates sin. Psalm 89:32 says, "Then I will punish their transgression with the rod, and their iniquity with stripes." God will punish sin. Read Romans 1:8, 2:5; Ephesians 5:6; and Colossians 3:6. What do you see in these passages concerning God's punishment of sin? (See p. 80.)

_____

_____

_____

3. "For all have sinned and come short of the glory of God," Paul wrote in Romans 3:23. Summarize what each of the first three chapters of Romans says about sin. (See pp. 80-81.)

_____

_____

_____

_____

"The just shall live by faith was the watchword of the Protestant Reformation" (p. 78).

4. In Romans 3, Paul "brings the new revelation of the mercy of God." What is the nature of His mercy described in Romans 3:21-24? (See p. 77.)

_____

_____

_____

_____

_____

"The doctrine of justification condemns every effort on the part of man to justify himself. It is God that justifies—not man" (p. 81).

5. The Westminster Catechism, Question and Answer 33, defines justification as "an act of God's free grace, wherein He pardons all our sins, and accepts us as righteous in His sight, only for the righteousness of Christ imputed to us, and received by faith alone." What is the first point you note in this definition? What Scripture verses from Romans 3 support this point? (See p. 81.)

_____

_____

_____

_____

6. Why is it important for us to understand that justification is "an act—not a process?" (See pp. 81-82.)

_____

_____

_____

7. Is justification an activity that is "internal" or "external" to us? Explain this. (See pp. 81-82.)

_____

_____

> "Justify does not mean to make holy. . . . It is a declaration about a person—not a change of his internal nature" (p. 82).

_____

_____

_____

8. What are the two parts of the work of Christ for us? (See p. 83.)

_____

_____

_____

_____

9. If justification does not make us holy, how does it allow us to stand before God? (See pp. 82-83.)

_____

_____

_____

_____

10. How is the doctrine of justification different from forgiveness? (See pp. 83-84.)

_____

_____

_____

_____

_____

"If, as some suppose, justification were to be identified merely with forgiveness of sins, then we would merely be forgiven and brought to the place that Adam started. We would still have to work out our own righteousness, which Adam with his perfect nature was unable to do" (p. 83).

11. How can we picture ourselves as righteous in Christ? (See pp. 85-86. Also read Isaiah 61:10.)

_____

_____

_____

LEVEL TWO QUESTIONS

1. Have you ever felt the weight of guilt so intensely that you had no peace? Have you ever felt as if your sins were too great to be forgiven?

_____

_____

_____

2. Have you tried to find peace and payment for the guilt of your sins by doing good works? Do you know someone who even now is in that position?

_____

_____

_____

3. How does knowing that justification is entirely the act of God change your thinking and your feelings about your guilt?

_____

_____

_____

4. Why do you think it is important for us to understand that justification is an act that is external to us?

_____

_____

_____

_____

5. In the past, when you thought of Christ's work of redemption, what have you focused on most? How does it change your thinking about your redemption to consider that His obedience to God was both active and passive?

_____

_____

_____

_____

_____

6. Would you say that you are living in the reality of your justification?

_____

_____

_____

_____

7. Dr. Kennedy stated in this chapter that "the doctrine of justification is the Gospel of our Lord Jesus." Martin Luther stated that "in it [justification] are involved all other articles of our faith." How would you explain these statements?

_____

_____

_____

LEVEL THREE QUESTIONS

1. What is the most transforming truth you have learned concerning the doctrine of justification through this study? Who do you want to tell about this truth?

_____

_____

_____

_____

2. Some people speak of "guarding their righteousness." What do you think of this statement? Is there any action that you believe you should take in order to walk in accordance with the transforming truth of your justification by God's grace?

_____

_____

_____

_____

3. Do you have a friend who is burdened by a sense of guilt and shame for sin? What have you learned through your study of this chapter that you can share with him or her?

_____

_____

_____

_____

4. The following prayer is one you may want to share with this friend.

> Enlighten me, O Lord, that I may see myself as I really am, despise my sins, trust not in my own righteousness, but flee to Your Cross. Cleanse me by Your blood, O Christ, that I may be clothed in Your righteousness, justified from all my sins, and fit to enter eternal life in Heaven with You. In your blessed name I pray. Amen.

ANSWERS TO LEVEL ONE QUESTIONS

QUESTION 1: We must recognize 1) the reality of our sin and guilt, and 2) the reality of God's wrath upon us for our sin.

QUESTION 2: Romans 1:18: "For the wrath of God is revealed from heaven against all ungodliness and unrighteousness of men, who suppress the truth in unrighteousness."
Romans 2:5: "But in accordance with your hardness and your impenitent heart you are treasuring up for yourself wrath in the day of wrath and revelation of the righteous judgment of God."
Ephesians 5:6: "Let no one deceive you with empty words, for because of these things the wrath of God comes upon the sons of disobedience."
Colossians 3:6: "Because of these things the wrath of God is coming upon the sons of disobedience." These passages all describe the certainty of God's wrath upon sin.

QUESTION 3: In Romans 1, Paul speaks of the sin of the Gentiles, which makes them worthy of condemnation. In Romans 2, Paul speaks of the sin of the Jews, which makes them worthy of condemnation. In Romans 3, Paul speaks of the sin of both the Jews and Gentiles—there is no difference. Both are worthy of condemnation.

QUESTION 4: Romans 3:21-24: "But now the righteousness of God apart from the law is revealed, being witnessed by the Law and the Prophets, even the righteousness of God, through faith in Jesus Christ, to all and on all who believe. For there is no difference; for all have sinned and fall short of the glory of God, being justified freely by His grace through the redemption that is in Christ Jesus." God's righteousness is revealed, which is through faith in Jesus Christ. It is on all who believe; both Jew and Gentile. It is freely given through Jesus, not by any work of the law.

QUESTION 5: Justification is an act of God. It is not anything that we do. Romans 3:21—"righteousness of God," 3:22—"righteousness of God," 3:24—"justified freely by His grace."

QUESTION 6: It is important to understand that justification is an act, not a process, because it is a one-time event. Furthermore, it is complete and perfect forever. It is an act of God's grace. We are not justified by anything that we are doing on an ongoing basis; it is purely by the "grace and unmerited favor of God."

QUESTION 7: Justification is external to us. It is something that is declared about us. It does not change our heart. (God does that through His Spirit by regeneration and sanctification.) Justification is the act of God declaring us righteous.

QUESTION 8: The two parts to the work of Christ are: 1) His active obedience in perfectly obeying every command of God, and 2) His passive obedience in enduring the sufferings of the Cross to take away all our sins by paying the punishment for them.

QUESTION 9: Justification does two things that allow us to stand before God: 1) It constitutes us as righteous in His sight by imputing to us the righteousness of Jesus Christ, and 2) It declares that the demands of the law have all been fulfilled through Christ; therefore, we are no longer guilty and deserving of punishment for any of our sins.

QUESTION 10: Justification is infinitely greater than forgiveness. Forgiveness gives pardon for sins, but it does not make us righteous. We can only stand before God in a right relationship with Him, if we are righteous in His sight. That is only possible if Christ's righteousness is imputed to us. Then we can be assured that when God looks at us, He sees Christ's accomplished work, both active and passive, by which God has constituted us righteous and declared us righteous in His sight.

QUESTION 11: In Matthew 22:1-13, Jesus speaks of the man who was not wearing a wedding garment, and thus was cast into outer darkness. Isaiah 61:10 tells us that God clothes us with "the garments of salvation, . . . the robe of righteousness." What a beautiful picture this gives us of how we are clothed with Christ's righteousness through justification by faith in Him!

Isaiah 61:10

> I will greatly rejoice in the LORD,
> My soul shall be joyful in my God;
> For He has clothed me with the garments of salvation,
> He has covered me with the robe of righteousness,
> As a bridegroom decks himself with ornaments,
> And as a bride adorns herself with her jewels.

ENDNOTE:

1   Bouman, Herbert J. A. (1955), "The Doctrine of Justification in the Lutheran Confessions," *Concordia Theological Monthly*, Vol. XXVI, No. 11, Nov. 1955, p. 801.

9

Sanctification

INTRODUCTION

As Christians, we claim that our faith is based on truth. Faith believes the truth we have received. If we are to ground our actions in truth, we must understand the truths we believe. Historically, the Church has stated the truths it holds as doctrines, dogmas, or creeds. "Christianity, indeed, is not only life, it is also doctrine," wrote Dr. Kennedy in this chapter. Doctrine comes from the Latin word for "to teach" and dogma comes from the Greek word for "to think." Would any of us not want to be taught by God's Word? Would any of us not want to think carefully about what God's Word teaches us?

As you study the doctrine of sanctification, think of what you believe concerning your sanctification. Are you living according to that belief? If you see some inconsistency in what you think and how you are acting in regard to your sanctification, maybe there is a lack of clarity in what you believe. Is it time to develop a clearer understanding of the doctrine of sanctification?

LEARNING OBJECTIVES

- To learn the biblical view of the doctrine of sanctification.
- To learn the difference between justification and sanctification.
- To learn what Scripture teaches concerning holiness in the life of the Christian.
- To respond with head, heart, and will to the scriptural teaching and understanding of sanctification.

LEVEL ONE QUESTIONS

1. The Reformers saw confusion in the teachings of the Roman Catholic Church between the doctrine of sanctification and the doctrine of justification. Explain the basic differences between these two doctrines. (See pp. 89-90.)

_____

_____

_____

2. Justification and sanctification both deal with different aspects of our sin. What are these two aspects? (See p. 90.)

_____

_____

_____

3. How does God deal with these two aspects of our sin through justification and sanctification? (See pp. 90-91.)

_____

_____

_____

_____

"Instead of guilt, what we need is righteousness in the sight of the law; instead of corruption, what we need is holiness" (p. 91).

4. Why do we need holiness? (See pp. 91-92.)

_____

_____

_____

"In English the word holiness comes from the word whole—wholeness, soundness, holiness" (p. 91).

5. Habakkuk 1:13a speaks of God's holiness: "You are of purer eyes than to behold evil, and cannot look on wickedness." What Scripture speaks of our need to be holy? (See p. 92.)

"God calls us to holiness in body, mind, and spirit. Anything which is contrary—any rottenness, any corruption—God demands that it be replaced by that which is sound and holy" (pp. 92-93).

_____

_____

_____

_____

6. What does I John 2:16-17 show us about the sources of unholiness in this world? (See p. 92.)

_____

_____

_____

_____

_____

7. How do we receive holiness? (See p. 93.)

_____

_____

_____

8. What are the five means of sanctification we have been given? (See p. 93.)

_____

_____

_____

_____

"Let me remind you that you could read the Word of God until you were green in the face, and you could pray until your knees were worn smooth, and you would not be sanctified one bit, if the Holy Spirit of God did not sanctify you" (p. 94).

9. What is the instrument that we must use to receive the sanctification of the Holy Spirit? (See p. 94.)

_____

_____

_____

_____

_____

10. Is any part of our sanctification the result of our own works? (See pp. 93-94.)

_____

_____

_____

> "The agent of sanctification is not man but the Holy Spirit. It is the infusing of the holiness of Christ. There is no holiness in us. A rotten apple could jump up and down, bestir itself, clap its hands, and do whatever it wanted to, and it would still be nothing more than a rotten apple. Likewise, there is nothing about ourselves that can make us holy" (p. 93).

LEVEL TWO QUESTIONS

1. Prior to studying this chapter, what was your view of the way Christians are to become holy?

_____

_____

_____

2. Do you see a disparity between the emphasis placed upon the doctrine of justification and the doctrine of sanctification within your church? If so, which doctrine is given more attention?

_____

_____

_____

_____

3. Now that you have studied this chapter, how would you respond to the person who claims that he or she "is holy?"

_____

_____

_____

_____

> "There is the need of faith, realizing that we cannot sanctify ourselves, realizing that God demands holiness of us, realizing that we are incapable of producing it" (p. 94).

4. Is there a particular area of your life where you see a need for greater holiness?

_____

_____

_____

5. Some have said that there is no longer any sense of the "sacred" in our society. How would you explain this in relation to the holiness of God?

_____

_____

_____

6. In what ways does our culture and society promote unholiness? Consider 1 John 2:16-17 in your response.

_____

_____

_____

> "For all that is in the world—the lust of the flesh, the lust of the eyes, and the pride of life—is not of the Father but is of the world. And the world is passing away, and the lust of it; but he who does the will of God abides forever" (1 John 2:16-17).

7. Prior to your study of this chapter what was your view of the importance of the means of sanctification (see p. 93.) and the work of the Holy Spirit in your sanctification?

_____

_____

_____

8. What is your view now?

_____

_____

_____

"Would you know the holiness of God? Then you will have to know Him who is holy; for apart from Him, the thrice-holy God, there is nothing in this sin-tainted world but death and corruption. Draw near unto Him. Spend time with Him. Reach out in faith unto Him, and you will come to know the blessings of God's holiness and the meaning of His sanctification" (p. 94).

LEVEL THREE QUESTIONS

1. Do you think you are fully utilizing the means of sanctification that were identified in this chapter? If not, what changes are you going to make?

_____

_____

_____

2. How can you encourage your spouse or family members or other Christians to desire greater holiness and to be more active in their sanctification through the means of sanctification?

_____

_____

_____

3. What have you learned through your study of this chapter that you can share with a neighbor or an acquaintance who is seeking holiness?

_____

_____

_____

4. What can you share with a family member, friend, or fellow worker who is living an unholy life?

_____

_____

_____

_____

O God, deliver us, we pray, from a corrupted view of Your holiness. May we never forget that You have said, "Be holy, for I am holy...." You are the altogether Holy One. O Lord, teach us to despise our sin and corruption, our vileness and rottenness, and may we reach unto You, O Source of purity and holiness, that we may be healed and made whole in body, mind, and soul. We pray this in the name of Christ. Amen

ANSWERS TO LEVEL ONE QUESTIONS

QUESTION 1: Justification is an act which takes place once and for all and is complete. It is external to us. It is something that is declared about us: We are not guilty and able to stand righteous before God. Sanctification is a process which lasts from the beginning of the Christian life until the moment we die. Sanctification is internal. It is the ongoing change that takes place in our heart and life through the work of the Holy Spirit.

QUESTION 2: There are two aspects to sin: 1) guilt, which is liability to punishment under God's law, and 2) corruption, which is the effect of sin on our nature.

QUESTION 3: Justification deals with the matter of our external relation to the law (our guilt) by declaring us righteous and imputing to us the righteousness of Christ. Sanctification deals with our internal corruption. It is the gradual infusion of the holiness of Christ into us.

QUESTION 4: We need holiness because we are totally corrupt, rotten, and sinful by nature. Because we are separated from God, the only source of holiness, we are like rotten fruit that has been cut off the vine and fallen to the ground. We need the holiness of Jesus Christ; we need wholeness, soundness, and oneness.

QUESTION 5: Leviticus 11:44a states, "For I am the LORD your God. You shall therefore consecrate yourselves, and you shall be holy; for I am holy."

QUESTION 6: There is unholiness due to the lust of the flesh, the lust of the eyes, and the pride of life. None of these are godly. All of these will pass away with the passing away of this world.

QUESTION 7: We are sanctified by the work of God. The Holy Spirit infuses into us the holiness of Christ. There is no holiness in us apart from Him.

QUESTION 8: We have been given five means of sanctification: a) the Word of God, b) prayer, c) obedience to all of God's commandments, d) the sacraments, and e) worship. "The Holy Spirit takes our use of these means and makes them the method by which He sanctifies us" (pp. 93-94).

QUESTION 9: We must use the instrument of faith to "reach out and take hold of God," crying out to Him to sanctify us and make us pure and cleanse us from our sins. We cannot sanctify ourselves; therefore we must trust in the Giver of grace and the Sanctifier of people, the Holy Spirit of God.

QUESTION 10: Although we make use of the means of grace—prayer, study of the Word of God, obedience, the sacraments, and worship—none of these can make us holy *per se*. It is ultimately the work of the Holy Spirit in and with our new nature.

10

Adoption

INTRODUCTION

Often those who have been adopted have a very special bond with their adoptive parents. They know that of all the babies or children their parents could have adopted, they chose them.

As you study this chapter on the doctrine of adoption, consider it in relation to the chapter on predestination. God, your heavenly Father, chose you to be His child. "For you did not receive the spirit of bondage again to fear, but you received the Spirit of adoption by whom we cry out, 'Abba, Father'" (Romans 8:15).

LEARNING OBJECTIVES

- To learn the biblical view of the doctrine of adoption.
- To learn what Scripture teaches us concerning our ability to please God.
- To learn what Scripture teaches concerning man's ability to do good.
- To respond with head, heart, and will to the scriptural teaching and understanding of human agency.

LEVEL ONE QUESTIONS

1. The doctrine of adoption has been ignored by many theologians. Even Reformers Calvin and Luther gave it little or no attention, and yet the Westminster Confession of Faith speaks of it in Chapter XII, stating that all those who are justified are also made:

> . . . partakers of the grace of adoption, by which they are taken into the number, and enjoy the liberties and privileges of the children of God, have His name put upon them, receive the Spirit of adoption, have access to the throne of grace with boldness, are enabled to cry, Abba, Father, are pitied, protected, provided for, and chastened by Him, as by a father: yet never cast off, but sealed to the day of redemption; and inherit the promises, as heirs of everlasting salvation.

What are three reasons Dr. Kennedy gives for the importance of the study of the doctrine of adoption? (See p. 97.)

_____

_____

_____

_____

2. What is the teaching of universalism? Is there any scriptural support for this teaching? (See p. 98.)

_____

_____

_____

"I suppose many Christians believe the doctrine of the fatherhood of God and the brotherhood of man to be biblical. This merely proves Hitler's dictum: Tell a lie which is big enough, tell it loud enough and often enough, and you can get most people to believe it" (p. 98).

3. What is the state of natural man born into this world? (See pp. 98-99.)

_____

_____

_____

4. How do we become sons of God? (See p. 99.)

_____

_____

_____

5. State the three ways the term "sons of God" is used in Scripture. (See p. 99.)

_____

_____

_____

"The deception of the devil may be that all people are the sons of God and that He is Father of all, but this is not the teaching of the Scriptures" (p. 99).

6. Why is it important for us to understand the twofold relationship that Adam had with God before the fall? (See pp. 99-100.)

_____

_____

_____

7. What is the twofold remedy that had to be provided for man's condition after Adam's fall? (See pp. 100-101.)

_____

_____

_____

_____

8. In what two ways must man be restored to a relationship as a son of the heavenly Father? (See p. 101.)

_____

_____

_____

"People say that God created people because He was lonely. They fail to realize that God is the absolute, perfect Person; the three Persons of the Triune God have never been lonely. God did not create man because He was lonely; He created man for His own glory" (pp. 101-102).

_____

9. What is the difference between punishment and chastisement? (See p. 102.)

_____

_____

_____

_____

10. In what ways is the teaching of universalism a false doctrine of redemption? (See pp. 102-103.)

_____

_____

_____

_____

_____

11. What benefits do we have as God's adopted children? (See pp. 103-104.)

_____

_____

_____

_____

_____

_____

_____

"Christ, the suffering Servant and suffering Son, comes and provides for us not only our justification and restoration to the kingdom of God, but also our adoption and reclamation into the family of God. This is the great biblical doctrine of adoption" (p. 103).

LEVEL TWO QUESTIONS

1. Christians are often considered "intolerant" because we do not accept the belief that everyone is a child of God and part of His family (universalism). This idea has been used in school systems to promote a particular social or political agenda. How would you respond if you found the ideas of universalism being used in this way?

_____

_____

_____

_____

2. The truth concerning the natural state of man often causes offense when it is stated. It also divides those who are sons of God by adoption from those who are sons of the devil by birth into his kingdom. Is there any way we can avoid "giving offense" to those who are still under the control of the "prince of the power of the air," as Ephesians 2:2 states? (See Matthew 10:16.)

_____

_____

_____

_____

"The concept of the universal fatherhood of God and universal brotherhood of man is utterly foreign to the Scriptures" (p. 98).

3. As citizens of the kingdom of God and sons in God's household, there is nothing we should lack or need. Are you living in the full acknowledgment and recognition of the rights and privileges you have as both a heavenly citizen and a beloved son?

_____

_____

_____

_____

4. Do you have a filial disposition toward God? What is the quality of your relationship with God as your heavenly Father? What things have strengthened that relationship in your Christian life and walk?

_____

_____

_____

_____

5. How does the description of the difference between punishment and chastisement help you understand events in your life since you have become a Christian? Can you look back and see how there was chastisement to deal with the presence of a fault and to increase your holiness?

_____

_____

_____

_____

6. What benefits of adoption can you point to in your life?

_____

_____

_____

LEVEL THREE QUESTIONS

1. In completing this study of the doctrine of adoption, can you say that your relationship with God as your Father has been transformed in any way? If so, how has it changed?

_____

_____

_____

_____

2. What are benefits that we have through our adoption into God's family that you can share with your spouse, family members, or other Christians?

_____

_____

_____

_____

3. What can you share with a family member or friend who is struggling with feeling isolated and alone? What can you tell them that may be used by the Holy Spirit to draw that person to Christ?

_____

_____

_____

_____

ANSWERS TO LEVEL ONE QUESTIONS

QUESTION 1: Three reasons we should study the doctrine of adoption are: 1) it is of immeasurable solace to the saints of God when calamity overwhelms and tribulation comes in like a flood, 2) it is a biblical doctrine—the great end to the doctrine of predestination, and 3) it is the theological point of contact with the twentieth century's great heresy—universalism.

QUESTION 2: The teaching of universalism is that there is a universal "fatherhood of God and brotherhood of man." This teaching is totally foreign to the Scriptures.

QUESTION 3: Natural man born into this world is a "disobedient child of the devil, under the wrath of God (John 8:44 and Ephesians 2:2).

QUESTION 4: We become sons of God by receiving Christ and being translated into the kingdom of God's dear Son (John 1:12).

QUESTION 5: The three uses of the term sons of God in Scripture are: 1) Adam, the first man, was originally God's son (Luke 3:38); 2) there is the adoptive sense in which all believers are sons of God through faith in Jesus Christ (Galatians 3:26); 3) a third sense is a restrictive sense: Jesus Christ is the Son of God, the eternal Second Person of the Trinity and He has forever been the Son of God.

QUESTION 6: It is important for us to understand the two-fold relationship that Adam had with God before the fall in order to understand the completeness of our redemption. Before the fall, Adam was a member of the divine kingdom; God was his Sovereign and his Lord. Adam was also a member of God's created family; God was his father and friend.

QUESTION 7: The two-fold remedy that had to be provided for man's condition after Adam's fall must include restoration of our citizenship in God's kingdom; this was accomplished through our justification. There must also be a restoration of our sonship in God's family and household; this was accomplished through our adoption.

QUESTION 8: God restores man to a relationship as a son of the heavenly Father by giving him a new filial position and giving him a filial disposition. In his filial position, man receives rights and privileges in the household of God. Man receives a new filial disposition when he is given a new heart and nature through the regeneration of the Holy Spirit through faith in Christ.

QUESTION 9: The difference between punishment and chastisement is that: 1) Punishment is retrospective—it looks backward to the broken law and is not done to make the criminal better. It is done because the transgressed law demands punishment. 2) Chastisement is prospective— it looks to the future. It is given not for a broken law, but for the presence of a fault. It is to make the child better.

QUESTION 10: Universalism is a false doctrine of redemption because it: 1) denies the need of an atonement, 2) reduces the Bible to the story of the Prodigal Son in which the father embraces the son without atonement or payment for sins. All that is required is "repentance" and "evidence of the desire to do better in the future."

QUESTION 11: The benefits of adoption include: 1) being brought into the family of God, 2) being given His name, 3) being made heirs by an act of God's grace, 4) the promise that we have His Spirit put within us, 5) God's pity for us as a Father, 6) God's provision for all our needs, 7) God watching over us, 8) God defending us from our enemies, 9) one day being taken by Christ to that mansion in glory that He has prepared for us, and 10) looking into the face of God, whom many fear, and saying, "Abba, Father" (Romans 8:15).

Assurance of Salvation

INTRODUCTION

I John 5:13 states, "These things I have written to you who believe in the name of the Son of God, that you may know that you have eternal life, and that you may continue to believe in the name of the Son of God." The assurance that we have eternal life is one of the greatest comforts we can have as Christians.

Why do we need this assurance? Art Murray claims that children who profess faith in Christ at a young age need to receive assurance of their salvation before they become teens. He notes that otherwise, they will often doubt the reality of their faith.[1]

"All who are going to Heaven know they are," Dr. Kennedy stated in this chapter. Do you have assurance of your salvation? Can you share with a friend how they can have this assurance too?

LEARNING OBJECTIVES

- To learn the biblical view of how we can receive assurance of salvation.
- To learn the benefits of having assurance of salvation.
- To respond with head, heart, and will to the scriptural teaching and understanding of assurance of salvation.

LEVEL ONE QUESTIONS

1. Just like the individuals who are described in the opening of this chapter, we can also know what will become of us when we die. Unlike those who follow other religions, followers of Christ have His words: "I am the resurrection and the life. He who believes in Me, though he may die, he shall live. And whoever lives and believes in Me shall never die" (John 11:25-26). What are two reasons that people who claim to be Christians do not have assurance of eternal life? (See p. 106.)

_____

_____

_____

2. What truth from the book of Romans transformed Martin Luther and gave him assurance of his salvation? (See p. 107.)

_____

_____

3. Eternal life is a gift. A gift is received in an instant. How can we receive this gift, according to John 1:12? "But as many as received Him, to them He gave the right to become children of God, to those who believe in His name." (See p. 108.)

_____

_____

_____

_____

"The Bible says that eternal life is a free gift from God. It is unearned, unworked for, unstriven for, unmerited, undeserved. It is a gift completely paid for by Christ and offered by His grace. Then how long does it take to obtain this gift? You merely reach out and take it" (p. 108).

4. At the Council of Trent the Roman Catholic Church declared, "Let that man who says he knows he has eternal life be anathema." What are two key Scriptures that this declaration contradicts? (See p. 108)

_____

_____

_____

_____

_____

_____

The Council of Trent convened three times between December 13, 1545, and December 4, 1563, in the city of Trent (modern Trento) as a response to the theological and ecclesiological challenges of the Protestant Reformation. It is considered one of the most important councils in the history of the Roman Catholic Church, clearly specifying the Catholic doctrines on salvation, the sacraments, and the biblical canon.

5. What is one of the greatest benefits the Christian has in knowing Christ and having assurance of salvation in Him? (See p. 108.)

_____

_____

_____

"It was this joy that enabled blind Fanny Crosby to write, 'Blessed assurance, Jesus is mine. O what a foretaste of glory divine!' No wonder many don't smile when they sing such a song. They are spiritually blind to the great truth it teaches!" (p. 109)

_____

_____

_____

6. What is a second benefit of having assurance of our salvation? (See p. 110.)

_____

_____

7. Good works can be the evidence of faith in Christ. But what difference is there in the motives for good works between the person who has assurance of eternal life and the one who does not know for sure if he or she is going to Heaven? (See pp. 110-111.)

_____

_____

8. What do Romans 8:16 and 1 John 5:10 tell us about those who have received the gift of eternal life? (See p. 111.)

_____

_____

_____

_____

LEVEL TWO QUESTIONS

1. Have you or someone close to you ever struggled with doubts about your eternal life? What have you learned in studying this chapter that has eliminated these doubts? What could you share with someone who is in doubt?

_____

_____

_____

2. Have you ever shared with someone that eternal life is a free gift? What was their response? Why do you think some find this difficult to accept?

_____

_____

_____

_____

"Did you receive a gift last Christmas? Did it take you twenty years to get it? Do you know whether or not you have it? So it is with eternal life! It is the greatest Christmas present God has ever given to the world. 'The gift of God is eternal life through Jesus Christ our Lord' (Romans 6:23)" (p. 108).

3. The great preacher Charles Spurgeon said he experienced great joy when he knew that he had received eternal life: "My soul was filled with joy. I could have danced all the way home." What expressions of joy can others see in your life due to the assurance that you have of eternal life?

_____

_____

_____

4. In addition to joy, our assurance of eternal life through Christ should lead to holy living. Is there an area of your life that has not yet been touched by the claim of Christ as your Savior and Lord ?

_____

_____

_____

_____

"Faith is but the hand of a beggar reaching out to receive the gift of a King. The motive then, for Christian living is not gain, but gratitude for the gift of eternal life. God begins by giving us everything!" (p. 111).

5. After your study of this chapter, death should not be a "leap into darkness," unless you have never received the free gift of eternal life. Having received it, you can sing, "Blessed assurance, Jesus is mine. O what a foretaste of glory divine." If you have not received that gift, you are invited here to pray the prayer below and receive freely from God what God freely offers to you through Jesus Christ His Son:

> Dear God, I acknowledge that I have been trying to enter Heaven by my own works; yet all my deeds are like filthy rags in Your eyes. Forgive me, grant me repentance, and give me Your grace to receive the free gift of eternal life through Jesus Christ. I place my trust in Him alone for my salvation. In Jesus' name alone I pray. Amen.

LEVEL THREE QUESTIONS

1. When you see other Christians showing great joy in their salvation, are you able to join in their rejoicing? Or do you find yourself envying them? How will you respond the next time this occurs?

_____

_____

_____

_____

_____

2. Is there joy evident in the fellowship of Christians you are a part of? What can you share with those with whom you fellowship to encourage them in rejoicing?

_____

_____

_____

_____

_____

3. What have you learned through your study of this chapter that you can share with a family member, friend, or fellow worker who has expressed a fear of death?

_____

_____

_____

_____

_____

_____

_____

ANSWERS TO LEVEL ONE QUESTIONS

QUESTION 1: Two reasons that people who claim to be Christians may not have assurance of eternal life are: a) they are not truly Christians, or b) they are trusting in their own works to save them. In such cases, before they can have assurance, these individuals need to trust in Jesus Christ alone for their hope of eternal life. In addition, there are some Christians who have trusted in Jesus Christ for eternal life, but do not understand what the Bible teaches about assurance of salvation. In these cases, you can show people the verses that speak of assurance, such as John 6:47 and I John 5:11-12.[2]

QUESTION 2: Martin Luther was transformed by the truth that "The just shall live by faith" (Romans 1:17), which gave him assurance of his salvation.

QUESTION 3: According to John 1:12, "But as many as received Him, to them He gave the right to become children of God, to those who believe in His name." We receive the gift of eternal life by receiving Jesus and believing in His name.

QUESTION 4: At the Council of Trent the Roman Catholic Church declared that "the man who *says he knows he has eternal life* [emphasis added] be anathema." This contradicts the following truths of Scripture:

> I John 5:13: "These things I have written to you who believe in the name of the Son of God, *that you may know that you have eternal life*, [emphasis added] and that you may continue to believe in the name of the Son of God."
> 2 Peter 1:10: "Therefore, brethren, be even more diligent *to make your call and election sure* [emphasis added], for if you do these things you will never stumble."

QUESTION 5: One of the greatest benefits the Christian has in knowing Christ and having assurance of salvation through Him, is our joy in Him and our salvation.

QUESTION 6: A second benefit of having assurance of our salvation is that it is "a wellspring of all Christian motives for holy living."

QUESTION 7: The difference in the motive for good works of the person who has assurance of eternal life and the one who does not know for sure if he or she is going to Heaven is as follows: The Bible clearly shows that: 1) even our "good works" are unacceptable to God, because our motives are wrong and "They that are in the flesh cannot please God" (Romans 8:8). 2) As long as we are at enmity with God and dead in our sins (Ephesians 2:1, 5) nothing we do is acceptable to Him as a "good work" (Isaiah 64:6).[3] But once we have received eternal life by trusting in Christ, all our good works are done out of gratitude for that marvelous gift of His love and grace.

QUESTION 8: 1 John 5:10 and Romans 8:16 tell us that the Spirit of God bears witness in us that we are the children of God.

> 1 John 5:10-12: "He who believes in the Son of God has the witness in himself; he who does not believe God has made Him a liar, because he has not believed the testimony that God has given of His Son. And this is the testimony: that God has given us eternal life, and this life is in His Son. He who has the Son has life; he who does not have the Son of God does not have life."
>
> Romans 8:16: "The Spirit Himself bears witness with our spirit that we are children of God."

ENDNOTES:

1 Murphy, A. (2000). *The Faith of a Child.* Chicago, IL: Moody Press, pp. 68-69.
2 Kennedy, D. J. (1996). *Evangelism Explosion.* Wheaton, IL: Tyndale House Publishers, pp. 82-83.
3 See Chapter Two, "Does Man Have Free Will?"

12

Good Works

INTRODUCTION

Bill Gates has given away billions of dollars to various good causes, such as the prevention of disease in developing nations and the care of those afflicted by AIDS. Does he have a better chance of getting into Heaven because of his enormous philanthropy?

What about Mother Theresa? Do you think God will let her into Heaven because she has rescued hundreds of thousands of street children from death and sickness? Just where do our good works fit into God's plan of salvation? At the beginning or at the end? Ephesians 2:8-10 states, "For by grace you have been saved through faith, and that not of yourselves; it is the gift of God, not of works, lest anyone should boast. For we are His workmanship, created in Christ Jesus for good works, which God prepared beforehand that we should walk in them." Why are you performing your good works?

LEARNING OBJECTIVES

- To learn the biblical view of good works.
- To learn what true good works are according to Scripture.
- To learn what Scripture teaches concerning the source of true good works.
- To learn the relation between good works and salvation.
- To respond with head, heart, and will to the scriptural teaching and understanding of good works.

LEVEL ONE QUESTIONS

1. Sanctification is the work of God the Holy Spirit within us. We are sanctified—set apart—by the Holy Spirit unto good works. (See 2 Timothy 2:20-21, Ephesians 2:8-10, Titus 3:8 and Philippians 2:13.) What is the relation between our sanctification by the Holy Spirit and the good works that we do as Christians? (See pp. 113-114.)

_____

_____

_____

_____

2. What is the first requirement of a good work in order to qualify as "good" in God's view? (See p. 114.)

_____

_____

_____

_____

_____

"Religions through the centuries have commanded people to do all sorts of human works that they invented as supposedly pleasing to God. But the only way to please God is to obey Him" (p. 114).

3. What is the first and foremost characteristic of a "good person"? (See p. 115.)

_____

_____

_____

_____

4. What should be the relation of the Christian to the law of God? What Scripture verse is applicable in this context? (See pp. 115-116.)

_____

_____

_____

_____

ANTINOMIANISM is the doctrine or belief that the Gospel frees Christians from required obedience to any law, whether scriptural, civil, or moral.

5. What is the second requirement for a work to be a "good work"? (See p. 116.)

_____

_____

_____

_____

"'A good tree cannot bear bad fruit, nor can a bad tree bear good fruit' (Matthew 7:18). It is impossible for the human heart in its natural, depraved, sinful state to ever bring forth anything that in the sight of God would be considered good" (p. 116).

6. Explain why the works we do must originate from a heart "purified by faith." (See p. 116.)

_____

_____

_____

_____

_____

"The reason unregenerate people cannot get to Heaven by their good works is not because they do not have enough, but because they don't have any! 'For whatsoever is not of faith is sin'" (Romans 14:23) (p. 117).

7. What is the third requirement for a work to be a good work? (See p. 118.)

_____

_____

_____

_____

8. Those who love "the praise of men more than the praise of God" (John 12:43) will never do any true good works. Why? (See p. 119.)

_____

_____

_____

9. Summarize the biblical teaching on the relation of good works and salvation. (See pp. 120-121.)

_____

_____

_____

_____

_____

"Do you have a good work? How foolish for unregenerate people to believe they can buy eternal life and earn their way to Heaven. Are we saved by these good works? Evidently no, because until we are saved, we do not possess one good work" (p. 120).

LEVEL TWO QUESTIONS

1. Have you ever forced yourself to do something because you thought it was "the right thing to do"? Do you think that such an action qualified as a good work?

_____

_____

_____

_____

2. This chapter has touched on several ethical systems that make claims for determining if an action is "good." Utilitarianism claims that what is useful is good; especially if it is directed toward achieving the greatest happiness for the greatest number of people. The doctrine of hedonism claims that pleasure or happiness is the highest good. Have you seen contexts where either of these two views has been used to argue that an action is good? How would you respond now to such an argument?

_____

_____

_____

_____

_____

> "The conscious, thoughtful, purposeful, directed end of our actions is always the glory of God. Any action which falls short of that glory is thereby not a good work and is sin" (p. 119).

3. Now that you have studied this chapter, how would you respond to the person who claims that he or she does many "good things"? (Also review what you wrote in response to Question 3 in the Level Two Questions of Chapter Two.)

_____

_____

_____

_____

4. In evaluating your own motives for doing good works, how would you measure yourself according to the three requirements identified for good works in this chapter? In what areas do you see the need for change?

_____

_____

_____

_____

> "Good works are absolutely the necessary result of a saving faith and the only evidence of it" (p. 121).

5. If you have found yourself lacking as you evaluated your motives, you may want to pray the following prayer:

> O God, help me to prove my faith by my works. Enable me to examine my heart. May Your glory be my only aim and goal. May all I do be done to Your glory and praise. Fill me with Your Holy Spirit so that I may do the works You have set before me through His power. I ask this in the name of Jesus Christ, who with the Father and the Holy Spirit, are the eternal and most Holy God, now and forevermore. Amen.

LEVEL THREE QUESTIONS

1. What activities in your church are you presently involved in? Is there a temptation in any of them to serve for the "praise of men" rather than God's glory? What can you do to ensure that you keep your aim and attitude of heart one of *Soli Deo Gloria* (To the glory of God alone)?

_____

_____

_____

_____

2. How can you encourage your spouse, family members, or other Christians to strive to do good works that glorify God and bring praise to Him, rather than personal recognition?

_____

_____

_____

_____

3. How does your church encourage people to serve in a manner that enables them to avoid the temptation of serving for the "praise of men"?

_____

_____

_____

_____

ANSWERS TO LEVEL ONE QUESTIONS

QUESTION 1: The relation between our sanctification by the Holy Spirit and the good works that we do as Christians is that sanctification is the work of the Holy Spirit within us. He makes us a new creature, creating a new nature, a new heart, and a holy disposition. Holiness is implanted within us. Our good works come out of our new nature by faith.

QUESTION 2: The first requirement of a good work in order to qualify as "good" in God's view is that it conforms to His divine law. Our good works must be pleasing to Him by obeying His commandments. "If you love me, keep my commandments" (John 14:15).

QUESTION 3: The first and foremost characteristic of a "good person" is that he or she is obedient to God's holy commandments.

QUESTION 4: The Christian's relation to the law of God should be one of loving obedience. Jesus Christ fulfilled the law and took the penalty of it, but the law of God is still the only transcript of the immutable will of God. "He who has My commandments and keeps them, it is he who loves Me. And he who loves Me will be loved by My Father, and I will love him and manifest Myself to him" (John 14:21).

QUESTION 5: The second requirement for a work to be a good work is that it be done from a heart purified by faith. "Without faith it is impossible to please God" (Hebrews 11:6). "Faith brings the Holy Spirit into the heart to cleanse, wash, purify, and work within us those holy inclinations and dispositions to do things which are truly pleasing to a Holy God" (p. 112).

QUESTION 6: The works we do must originate from a heart "purified by faith" because it is impossible for the human heart in its natural, depraved, sinful state to ever bring forth anything that in the sight of God would be considered good. "They that are in the flesh cannot please God" (Romans 8:8). As long as we are at enmity against God and dead in our sins (Ephesians 2:1, 5) nothing that we do is acceptable to Him as a "good work" (Isaiah 64:6).

QUESTION 7: The third requirement for a work to be a good work is that it is directed solely toward the glory of God. God made us for His own glory. The end of all our actions is to be to the glory of God.

QUESTION 8: The works of those who love "the praise of men more than the praise of God" (John 12:43) can never be true good works, because these works are directed toward their own egos and their own self-glorification. The essence of such works is sin.

QUESTION 9: In summary, the biblical teaching on the relation of good works and salvation is that: a) until we are saved, we do not possess one good work, b) once we are saved, our good works are the necessary consequence of our salvation and the evidence that we truly have faith, for "Thus also faith by itself, if it does not have works, is dead" (James 2:17).

13

Perseverance of the Saints

INTRODUCTION

Do you know anyone, or perhaps have a friend who thinks he or she needs to "get saved" again every time there is a revival or crusade in town? Interestingly, the question of whether a Christian can cease to be a Christian, and thus would need to become a Christian again, is generally answered in the same way by Lutherans as by Roman Catholics. It is also answered the same by all those whose theology has been influenced by Arminianism, including both Methodists and Pentecostals.

The teaching of the Roman Catholic Church is that a person may indeed be a Christian and then cease to be one. Likewise, the Lutherans, Methodists and Pentecostals all agree that a person may be saved and then lost.

Nevertheless, there is one group of churches that answers the question, "Can a person be saved and then lost?" with an emphatic "No!" That is the group that has followed the teaching of the Protestant Reformer John Calvin. The doctrine of perseverance of the saints is one that all Calvinists have historically held to, whether they were Reformed, Presbyterian, Baptist, Congregationalist, or Anglican. Although many of these churches no longer hold to this doctrine, due to the influence of Arminianism, an understanding of the doctrine of perseverance of the saints is one that can give the Christian believer great comfort.

Therefore, your careful study of this chapter may enable you to provide an answer to your friend the next time he or she is wondering whether to go forward to "get saved" again.

LEARNING OBJECTIVES

- To learn the biblical view of the doctrine of perseverance of the saints.
- To learn what Scripture teaches us concerning falling away and persevering to the end.
- To learn what Scripture teaches concerning justification and glorification.
- To respond with head, heart, and will to the scriptural teaching and understanding of perseverance of the saints.

LEVEL ONE QUESTIONS

1. In order to understand the doctrine of perseverance of the saints, we must understand that salvation is a gift through God's grace and faith in Jesus Christ. Given that salvation is a gift, what does Romans 11:29 tell us that helps us to understand why we can never lose that gift? (Reading this verse in several versions of the Bible may be helpful to understand its full meaning.) (See p. 125.)

_____

_____

_____

2. What are other terms that have been used for this doctrine? What emphasis is missed in the use of these other terms? (See pp. 125-126.)

_____

_____

_____

_____

3. Chapter XVII, Article I, of the Westminster Confession of Faith speaks of the perseverance of the saints as follows: "They, whom God hath accepted in his Beloved, effectually called, and sanctified by his Spirit, can neither totally nor finally fall away from the state of grace, but shall certainly persevere therein to the end, and be eternally saved." Who is the Confession speaking of in the reference "they?" (See p. 126.)

"The Bible says that those who persevere until the end shall be saved. It doesn't say that we may make a profession and then live for the world, the flesh, and the devil for years and then go to Heaven. Only those who persevere till the end are those who are going to Heaven" (p. 126).

4. In order to persevere to the end, we need someone to keep us. Who is able to do so? (See p. 126 and also I Thessalonians 5:23 and Jude I:I.)

---

5. What is the comfort that the doctrine of perseverance of the saints gives to the Christian who knows that he or she has been saved by God's grace? (See pp. 126-127.)

_____

_____

_____

"Can you say, 'I know that I have eternal life; I know that I'm in a state of grace'? If you cannot, then the subject we are discussing is of no value to you. You must first repent of your sins, cease to trust in your own good works, in your own strivings, and put your trust in Christ alone for your salvation" (p. 127).

6. Is it possible for a person to partially and temporarily fall away, though not totally and finally? What examples are there to support your answer? (See pp. 127-128 and also 1 John 2:19.)

_____

_____

_____

_____

7. Those that begin the Christian life on earth will end it in Heaven. Romans 8:30 says, "Whom He justified, these He also glorified." What is the relationship between justification and glorification? (See pp. 128-129.)

_____

_____

_____

_____

8. What is the great promise stated in John 10:29? (See p. 129.)

_____

_____

_____

_____

_____

9. There are two aspects to God's keeping us. On the one hand the omnipotent power of God keeps us and holds us in our salvation. If that were not true, none of us would persevere for one day (p. 126). On the other hand, God uses Scripture to keep us. How does He do so? (See pp. 130-132.)

_____

_____

_____

_____

_____

10. Explain how I Corinthians 9:27 and Romans 8:38-39 show the two sides to the doctrine of the perseverance of the saints. (See pp. 130-132.)

_____

_____

_____

_____

LEVEL TWO QUESTIONS

I. Have you (or someone you know) ever doubted whether you have truly been saved? Perhaps you have struggled with a sin in your life that seems to loom so large you doubt that you could be a child of God. Or maybe you consider your faith so small that it could not possibly be genuine. What have you learned thus far about the transforming truths of justification, sanctification, adoption, assurance, and now perseverance of the saints that can help you and others when these doubts arise?

_____

_____

_____

_____

2. Review again the teachings of Arminianism discussed in Chapter Three, "Effectual Calling." How do these teachings lead to the view that we can be saved and then lost? (Consider the two problems with Arminianism; its view of man and its view of God.)

"If the Gospel consisted of no more than an invitation, then Heaven indeed would be an empty place. As Spurgeon said, 'What good is a "whosoever will" in a world where everybody won't?' So the first problem with the Arminian view is that man is not free to do what he ought" (p. 46).

_____

_____

_____

_____

_____

3. Have you or someone you know ever partially or temporarily fallen away? What brought you back to the Lord? How can you pray for someone who has fallen away?

_____

_____

_____

4. Why do you think it is difficult for some in the Church to accept this doctrine of the perseverance of the saints? Do you have trouble accepting this doctrine?

_____

_____

_____

5. If you answered affirmatively in the previous question, consider how the doctrines of the sovereignty of God, predestination, and effectual calling are related to the doctrine of perseverance of the saints. In believing these doctrines, we are accepting that God is the One who selects us and draws us to Himself. If He has done that, He is able to keep us in relationship with Himself, regardless of the circumstances around us or our own human frailties. Do you see this as an encouragement to you? Can you encourage others by sharing these doctrines with them?

_____

_____

_____

_____

"It's as if it's all up to you, and that is all there is to it. But we know that behind the shadows in the dim unknown, there is Christ, who says, 'All that the Father gives me shall come to me' (John 6:37). None of those shall perish, for this is the Father's will. There is a God who has said that He has loved us from before the foundation of the world, that we have been predestinated eternally to be conformed to the image of His Son" (p. 131).

6. In the following chapter we will look at the promise of Christ's return. How might our persevering till the end be connected with the vision we hold of His return and our future glorification?

_____

_____

_____

LEVEL THREE QUESTIONS

1. Is there a family member, friend, or fellow worker with whom you want to share what you have learned in this chapter about persevering to the end?

_____

_____

2. What particular part of this chapter have you found most encouraging? Resolve to set this before yourself through memory or in a journal. Then when you face discouragements and trials, be reminded of the comfort we derive from the doctrine of the perseverance of the saints.

_____

_____

_____

ANSWERS TO LEVEL ONE QUESTIONS

QUESTION 1: Romans 11:29, "For the gifts and the calling of God are irrevocable," assures us that God will not take back or "revoke" His gift to us of eternal life. The definition of "irrevocable" is: not to be revoked or recalled; unable to be repealed or annulled; unalterable: an irrevocable decree.[1]

QUESTION 2: Other terms that have been used for this doctrine are "eternal security" or "once saved, always saved." Both of these terms fail to emphasize: a) the persevering aspect whereby we are enabled to continue steadfastly and maintain a purpose in spite of difficulty, obstacles, or discouragement, and b) the *saints* aspect. Those who persevere are those who have been predestined, called, justified, sanctified, and adopted into God's household. One would not expect those who are not saints in this sense to persevere in faith.

QUESTION 3: Chapter XVII, Article 1 of the Westminster Confession of Faith states: "They, whom God hath accepted in his Beloved, effectually called, and sanctified by his Spirit, can neither totally nor finally fall away from the state of grace, but shall certainly persevere therein to the end, and be eternally saved." "They" refers to "the saints" who are identified in the following phrase as those "whom God hath accepted in his Beloved, effectually called, and sanctified by his Spirit."

QUESTION 4: Only our omnipotent powerful God is able to keep us until the end! 1 Thessalonians 5:23: "Now may the God of peace Himself sanctify you completely; and may your whole spirit, soul, and body be preserved blameless at the coming of our Lord Jesus Christ." Jude 1:1: "To those who are called, sanctified by God the Father, and preserved in Jesus Christ."

QUESTION 5: The doctrine of perseverance of the saints gives comfort to the Christian who knows that he or she has been saved by God's grace, because we know that we will never "fall" from that state of grace. Our sins, shortcomings, and errors will be forgiven when we turn to Him in repentance. We can rejoice that we have eternal life and that Christ will never let us go!

QUESTION 6: It is possible for a person to partially and temporarily fall away, though not totally and finally. We see the example of Peter, who even denied Christ. Yet he was kept by Christ and was brought back to become a faithful servant of the Lord. Judas, however, did not have a new nature. He was not a true believer. In fact he was a child of the devil, and ultimately that was revealed in his actions and death. (See 1 John 2:19: "They went out from us, but they were not of us; for if they had been of us, they would have continued with us; but they went out that they might be made manifest, that none of them were of us.")

QUESTION 7: Justification is the work God does in declaring us righteous in Christ. It is the first thing that happens to us on earth when we are pardoned for our sins and clothed with the righteousness of Christ. Glorification is the first thing that happens to Christians in Heaven, when every trace of sin is removed and we are made "absolutely pure and holy, fit to stand in the presence of God." These two are connected, for as Romans 8:30 states, "whom He justified, these He also glorified."

QUESTION 8: John 10:29 states, "My Father, who has given them to Me, is greater than all; and no one is able to snatch them out of My Father's hand." This verse gives us a great promise, for our Father is holding us in His hand, and no one can take us out of it. This is the reason we can persevere until He takes us to Heaven!

QUESTION 9: On the one hand the omnipotent power of God keeps us and holds us in our salvation. If it were not for this, none of us would persevere for even one day. On the other hand, God uses Scripture to keep us by giving us warnings, such as 1 Corinthians 10:12, "Therefore let him who thinks he stands take heed lest he fall," and 1 Corinthians 9:27, "But I discipline my body and bring it into subjection, lest, when I have preached to others, I myself should become disqualified." These admonitions are "moral means" to keeping us until the end. God also chastens us when we fall, so that we will return to the path of obedience.

QUESTION 10: We see the two sides to the doctrine of the perseverance of the saints in 1 Corinthians 9:27, which shows how God keeps us by moral means and warnings on the path of obedience to Him. Also Romans 8:38-39 shows us His matchless love and grace that sustains us through any circumstance or situation, for "neither death nor life, nor angels nor principalities nor powers, nor things present nor things to come, nor height nor depth, nor any other created thing, shall be able to separate us from the love of God which is in Christ Jesus our Lord."

ENDNOTE:
1 irrevocable. Dictionary.com. *Dictionary.com Unabridged (v 1.1).* Random House, Inc.
   http://dictionary.reference.com/browse/irrevocable (accessed: October 19, 2007).

14

He Shall Come Again

INTRODUCTION

Do you long to see your Savior's face? For those who know Jesus Christ as their Lord and Savior, our longing for His return increases with our sanctification. However, for those who do not know Jesus Christ as their Savior and Lord, His return will be a frightening event! As 2 Thessalonians 1:7-8 describes it, this will be the time "when the Lord Jesus is revealed from heaven with His mighty angels, in flaming fire taking vengeance on those who do not know God, and on those who do not obey the gospel of our Lord Jesus Christ."

Even as Christ's testimony that "you will see the Son of Man sitting at the right hand of the Power, and coming with the clouds of heaven" caused the high priest to tear his garments in disbelief, there are those today who figuratively "tear their garments" at this doctrine. But we have the prophecy in Romans 14:10-12:

> For we shall all stand before the judgment seat of Christ.
> For it is written: "As I live, says the LORD,
> Every knee shall bow to Me,
> And every tongue shall confess to God."

So then each of us shall give account of himself to God. How can there be any doubt that He shall come again?

LEARNING OBJECTIVES

- To learn the biblical view of the doctrine of Christ's return.
- To learn what Scripture teaches us concerning Christ's bodily return, His visible return, His glorious return, His triumphant return, and His unexpected return.
- To respond with head, heart, and will to the scriptural teaching and understanding of Christ's return.

LEVEL ONE QUESTIONS

1. The return of Christ has been affirmed in the historic creeds of Christendom. List these. (See p. 133.)

_____

_____

_____

> The return of Christ "is found in all of the systematic theologies, the lectionaries, and the hymnals of all of the Christian Churches of history. It is part of the great faith of Jesus Christ! He shall come again!" (p. 133).

2. There are numerous prophesies concerning Christ's return in the Old Testament, and Christ Himself testified of it. The apostles wrote of it in the epistles. List some of the Scriptures that speak of Christ's return. (See pp. 133-134.)

_____

_____

_____

_____

"This second advent of Christ is the great hope of the Christian. It is to be the final culminating point of history—the great climacteric of the ages. When the last page of the last volume of history shall have been written, there shall be the final exclamation point: Jesus Christ shall come again! He shall appear in all of His glory in the sky. And in that day the drama of the ages shall be brought to a glorious conclusion" (p. 134).

3. The second advent of Christ is "the great hope of the Christian." What are four things we know concerning what it will *not* be like? (See p. 135.)

_____

_____

_____

_____

4. What are the five characteristics of Christ's coming which the Scriptures affirm? Identify these truths and cite key Scriptures that state them. (See pp. 135-139. Note: Although a number of Scriptures are listed in the text of *Truths That Transform*, you can use Bible software or a concordance to locate others that are only alluded to in this chapter.)

_____

_____

_____

_____

_____

_____

_____

5. What is the difference between those who will see Christ's return with terror and alarm and fear and trembling and those who look forward to Christ's return with joyful anticipation of seeing their Savior's face? (See p. 140.)

_____

_____

_____

_____

> "Has He come into your heart? Have you opened the door of that heart and said, 'Come, Lord Jesus, there is room in my heart for Thee'? If so, then that will be the day of days—the day of delight. You will see your Beloved, your long-sought Beloved, face to face" (p. 140).

6. On that day, what will be the word that will roar through the souls of those who never received Jesus as their Savior? What is the word that believers will rejoice to hear? (See p. 141.)

_____

_____

_____

LEVEL TWO QUESTIONS

1. There are many who think of Christ's return in terms of the fictionalized accounts of the *Left Behind* series of novels and films. (In reference to this series, Dr. Kennedy once said, "I'd rather get my theology from the Bible than from a novel!") How do you think the Church universal would benefit from a stronger focus on Christ's return?

_____

_____

_____

2. What are some of the negative results that have occurred when people thought they had identified the exact date of Christ's return?

_____

_____

_____

"All of your plans—your carefully laid plans for what you are going to do next week, next month, next year, the next decade, your plans for retirement—may all disappear in an instant should Christ appear today. Unexpectedly, He will come. Like a thief in the night, He will come" (p. 139).

3. Why should we know and tell others of the five truths that the Bible teaches about Christ's return?

_____

_____

_____

_____

4. In what ways do you find the knowledge of the five truths concerning Christ's return encouraging?

_____

_____

_____

_____

5. Have you ever dreamed of Christ's return or tried to imagine it, based on the Bible's descriptions? By using our imaginations to picture that glorious event, we may increase our sense of the reality and certainty of it. Write as full a description as you can of Christ's return—bodily, visibly, unexpectedly, in glory and triumph.

(The space below may not be sufficient. Do not limit yourself to it.

If you prefer, use your favorite art medium to provide a picture of Christ's return.)

LEVEL THREE QUESTIONS

1. Since Christ will return unexpectedly, we should keep the thought of His return uppermost in our thinking. What can you do to daily keep that thought before you?

_____

_____

_____

2. Is there someone in your family or among your friends and fellow workers who you know would be encouraged by your sharing the five truths concerning Christ's return with them? When can you share these with that person?

_____

_____

_____

3. Do you know for sure that Christ will say "Come!" to you when He returns? How would you tell someone else of your assurance?

_____

_____

_____

_____

_____

4. If Christ were to return today, is there a person you know who does not have assurance that he or she would hear Christ say, "Come!" When do you plan to share with that person how one can know for sure they will be invited to come and join Christ in the heavenly banquet? (See Matthew 22:1-14.)

_____

_____

_____

ANSWERS TO LEVEL ONE QUESTIONS

QUESTION 1: The return of Christ has been affirmed in the historic creeds of Christendom, including: the Apostles' Creed, the Nicene Creed, the Constantinopolitan Creed, the Westminster Confession of Faith, the Thirty-nine Articles of the Anglicans, and the Augsburg Confession of the Lutherans.

QUESTION 2: Some of the Scriptures that speak of Christ's return are:
Matthew 26:64: "Jesus said to him, 'It is as you said. Nevertheless, I say to you, hereafter you will see the Son of Man sitting at the right hand of the Power, and coming on the clouds of heaven.'"
Titus 2:13: "...looking for the blessed hope and glorious appearing of our great God and Savior Jesus Christ...."
Philippians 3:20: "For our citizenship is in heaven, from which we also eagerly wait for the Savior, the Lord Jesus Christ...."
1 Thessalonians 3:13: "...so that He may establish your hearts blameless in holiness before our God and Father at the coming of our Lord Jesus Christ with all His saints."
1 Thessalonians 4:17: "Then we who are alive and remain shall be caught up together with them in the clouds to meet the Lord in the air. And thus we shall always be with the Lord."
2 Thessalonians 1:7: "...and to give you who are troubled rest with us when the Lord Jesus is revealed from heaven with His mighty angels...."
1 Peter 5:4: "...and when the Chief Shepherd appears, you will receive the crown of glory that does not fade away."

QUESTION 3: The second advent of Christ is "the great hope of the Christian." It should not be confused with nor equated to any of the following:
1) It is not the coming of Christ into our hearts by faith when we trust in Him for our salvation. That is a spiritual coming. His second coming will be physical.
2) It is not Christ's pouring out of His Spirit at Pentecost.
3) It is not our going to be with Christ at death.

4) It is not Christ's coming in any of the cataclysmic events of world history, such as the fall of Rome.

QUESTION 4: The Scriptures affirm the following five characteristics of Christ's second coming:
1) Christ will come bodily. Acts 1:11: "Men of Galilee, why do you stand gazing up into heaven? This same Jesus, who was taken up from you into heaven, will so come in like manner as you saw Him go into heaven."
2) Christ will come visibly. Revelation 1:7: "Behold, He is coming with clouds, and every eye will see Him."
3) Christ will come gloriously. 1 Thessalonians 4:16: "For the Lord Himself will descend from heaven with a shout, with the voice of an archangel, and with the trumpet of God. And the dead in Christ will rise first."
4) Christ will come triumphantly. 2 Thessalonians 1:8-9: "... in flaming fire taking vengeance on those who do not know God, and on those who do not obey the gospel of our Lord Jesus Christ. These shall be punished with everlasting destruction from the presence of the Lord and from the glory of His power."
5) Christ will come unexpectedly. 2 Peter 3:10: "But the day of the Lord will come as a thief in the night, in which the heavens will pass away with a great noise, and the elements will melt with fervent heat; both the earth and the works that are in it will be burned up."

QUESTION 5: What will separate those who will view Christ's return with terror, alarm, fear and trembling from those who will greet Him with great joy and gladness will be the experience of the new birth (John 3:5). Those who have been redeemed from their sins, justified, and made righteous, those who have trusted in Christ and have been born again through His Word and Spirit will look forward to His coming. Those who have not been redeemed will fear it.

QUESTION 6: Those who do not know Christ will tremble at the word "Go!" Those who love His appearing will rejoice at the word "Come!"

15

The Holy Spirit

INTRODUCTION

The different views concerning the Person and work of the Holy Spirit have divided churches and mission fields. Divisions over beliefs about the Holy Spirit have split up fellowships and even families. Yet the Apostle Paul exhorted the church in Ephesus to walk worthy of their calling, "endeavoring to keep the unity of the Spirit in the bond of peace" (Ephesians 4:3).

Without the power of the Holy Spirit at work in us, all our efforts to establish churches, preach the Gospel, and win the lost are worthless. Without His blessings, we are weak and powerless and our sanctification is empty. May this study of the Holy Spirit enlighten and encourage you. You are encouraged to consider His work in your life, as you study the scriptural truths set forth concerning who He is, what He does, and how we may experience His blessings.

LEARNING OBJECTIVES

- To learn the biblical view of the Person of the Holy Spirit.
- To learn what Scripture teaches us concerning the work of the Holy Spirit.
- To learn what Scripture teaches concerning the blessings of the Holy Spirit.
- To learn what Scripture teaches concerning how we may experience the Spirit's blessing.
- To respond with head, heart, and will to the scriptural teaching and understanding of the Holy Spirit.

LEVEL ONE QUESTIONS

1. Significantly, almost all the cults deny that the Holy Spirit is a Person. What four attributes are ascribed to the Holy Spirit by Scriptures that show us that He is a Person? (See p. 145. Your concordance or Bible study software can assist you in locating the Scriptures that are alluded to, but not specifically identified in this section.)

_____

_____

_____

_____

_____

> "…It is clearly seen in Scripture that the Holy Spirit is God. He is a person, the Third Person of the Godhead. We might note that in the Apostles' Creed there are three paragraphs. The first paragraph deals with the Father…the second deals with the Son. The third begins with an affirmation of our belief in the Holy Spirit" (p. 140).

2. There are four major works of the Holy Spirit, exclusive of His personal work in our lives. (These will be identified separately.) Identify these four major works and provide Scripture references for each of them. (See p. 147. Again, you may use your concordance or Bible study software to assist you in locating some of the Scriptures that are alluded to, but not specifically identified in this section.)

> "The entirety of Christian worship is built on the concept of the triune God: Father, Son, and Holy Spirit.
> Praise God, from whom all blessings flow:
> Praise Him all creatures here below;
> Praise Him above, ye heavenly host;
> Praise Father, Son and Holy Ghost" (p. 140).

_____

_____

_____

_____

_____

3. What are the works that the Holy Spirit does personally in our lives? (See pp. 147-150.)

_____

_____

_____

4. In Ephesians 5:18 we read, "And do not be drunk with wine, in which is dissipation; but be filled with the Spirit." The Word of God exhorts us to be filled with the Holy Spirit. Dr. Kennedy wrote in this chapter that he had previously compared our need of being filled with the Spirit to our being "leaky vessels." Though we are filled, we leak out this power and need to be refilled. Later, he determined that his illustration was inadequate, because the Holy Spirit is a Person and therefore cannot "leak" out of us. So the new illustration he gave is that of an air conditioner that is blowing fresh, cool air into the house and filling every room that has been opened. What is the key point Dr. Kennedy made by way of this illustration? (See pp. 151-152.)

_____

_____

_____

5. What steps should we take as we seek the filling of the Holy Spirit in every part of our mind, heart, and will? (See pp. 152-153.)

_____

_____

_____

_____

_____

6. For what purpose have we been given the Holy Spirit? (See p. 153.)

_____

_____

_____

LEVEL TWO QUESTIONS

1. What was your view of the Holy Spirit prior to studying this chapter?

_____

_____

_____

2. Did you think of the Holy Spirit as a Person? If not, how did that affect your relationship with Him?

_____

_____

_____

3. Now that you have studied this chapter, how would you respond to the person who says that he or she is "filled with the Spirit"?

_____

_____

_____

4. One of the works of the Holy Spirit is to testify of Christ. Have you seen this evidence of the filling of the Spirit in the lives of fellow Christians or in the life of your church?

_____

_____

_____

_____

"You can always tell a church or an individual that is filled with the Spirit of God. How? Because he is speaking, or that church is speaking much about Jesus Christ" (p. 151).

5. Meditate on the work of the Holy Spirit in creation, in the inspiration of the Bible, in the conception of Christ, and in the establishment of the Church. Now write below of the wondrous power of the Holy Spirit that fills you!

_____

_____

_____

_____

6. If you see a lack of the power and filling of the Holy Spirit in your life, review again the steps to allow the Holy Spirit to flood us with His power and joy that were identified in pages 152 and 153. Then pray the following prayer:

Oh, Christ, grant me the fullness of Your Spirit that I seek from You. Help me to determine this day that I am not going to just skim along, relying on my own power and abilities, but fill me with Your Spirit that I may live in the fullness and power, the love and joy and peace that only the Holy Spirit can give. Holy Spirit, cleanse me, fill me, lead me, use me for the glory of Christ's name and the building of the Father's kingdom. In Christ's name I pray, Amen.

LEVEL THREE QUESTIONS

1. Having studied the work of the Holy Spirit, how are you going to endeavor to keep the unity of the Spirit in the bond of peace, as we are exhorted to do in the fourth chapter of Ephesians?

_____

_____

_____

_____

2. How can you encourage your family members, friends, or fellow workers to seek the filling of the Holy Spirit in their lives?

_____

_____

_____

_____

_____

3. The benefits that the Holy Spirit gives to the life of the Christian are far beyond our measuring. The fruits of the Spirit alone are the object of envy for thousands. Yet, too often we barely acknowledge that we have them. Write a prayer of thanksgiving for the work of the Holy Spirit in your life. Then tell the story of His work to someone else, so that he or she may also come to Christ and receive the fullness of the blessings of the Holy Spirit today.

_____

_____

_____

_____

_____

ANSWERS TO LEVEL ONE QUESTIONS

QUESTION 1: The attributes ascribed to the Holy Spirit by Scriptures that show us that He is a Person include the following:
1) Intellect and mind—see I Corinthians 2:9-11.
2) Emotion—see Ephesians 4:30.
3) Volition or will—see Acts 13:2-4; 16:6.
4) Communication—see John 16:13-14; Acts 8:29; 21:11.
The Holy Spirit is a Divine Person, and efforts to lie to the Holy Spirit are equal to lying to God—see Acts 5:3-4.

QUESTION 2: The four major works of the Holy Spirit (exclusive of His personal work in our lives) and Scripture references for each of these works are:
1) The work of the Spirit at creation—see Genesis 1:1-2; Job 26:13; Psalm 104:29-30.
2) The work of the Holy Spirit in giving us the Scriptures—see 2 Timothy 3:16; 2 Peter 1:20-21.
3) The work of the Holy Spirit in bringing Christ into the world—see Matthew 1:18-20; Luke 1:34-35.
4) The work of the Holy Spirit in bringing into existence the Church—see Acts 2.

QUESTION 3: The works that the Holy Spirit does personally in our lives include:
1) The work of regeneration—see John 3:5-8; Titus 3:5-6.
2) The work of sanctifying us by purging and cleansing us from sin—see Romans 8:13; 2 Corinthians 3:17-18.

3) The Holy Spirit brings power into our lives—see Acts 1:8; Ephesians 3:16.
4) The Holy Spirit gives us the fruit of the Spirit—see Galatians 5:22-23.
5) The Holy Spirit gives us assurance—see Romans 8:15-16; Ephesians 1:13-15.
6) The Holy Spirit guides us and leads us—see Romans 8:14; Galatians 5:18.
7) The Holy Spirit testifies of Christ—see John 15:26; 16:12-14.

QUESTION 4: The key point Dr. Kennedy is making by way of his illustration of the Holy Spirit being like an air conditioner is that we don't need more of the Holy Spirit; the Holy Spirit wants more of us. We need to "throw open the doors" and let the Holy Spirit have access to every part of our "minds, our habits, our hearts, our affections, our will, our speech, our feet, our hands, and all else that we are—then let the Holy Spirit have control of all our lives" (p. 145). This is being "filled with the Spirit."

QUESTION 5: In order to allow the Holy Spirit to fill us so that every part of our mind, heart and will is flooded with His power and joy we need to:
a) Confess our sins. Confess those areas of our lives that we have closed off to His power, whatever they may be. b) Repent of our sins and turn from them and follow Christ as our Lord.
c) Ask God to fill us with the Holy Spirit—this is not the request of the non-Christian to send the Holy Spirit to regenerate our heart, but rather the request of the believer to be completely filled in "every part of our being with Him." d) Believe that God will do what Christ said—that the Father will give the Holy Spirit to them that ask Him. "If you then, being evil, know how to give good gifts to your children, how much more will your Father who is in heaven give the Holy Spirit to those who ask Him!" (Luke 11:13). e) Go out and live, knowing that we are empowered by the Spirit to serve Christ.

QUESTION 6: We have not been given the Spirit for our own enjoyment or "ecstasy." We have been given the Spirit that we might serve Christ, glorify His name, and build His kingdom on earth!

16

The Most Unpopular Subject in the World

INTRODUCTION

Have you talked to anyone lately about what Hell is like? One common view is that all the sinners will be enjoying themselves doing all the sinful things that sent them to Hell in the first place. Recently a friend heard a teenage girl express the idea that she would be "skateboarding through Hell, giving high fives to the devil!"

In some respects there seems to be a resurgence of interest in the subject of Hell. The History Channel has periodically aired a program on the history of the various views of Hell throughout the ages. Still, the title of this chapter, "The Most Unpopular Subject in the World," reflects the unwillingness of most people to talk about the possibility of spending their own eternal destiny in Hell. The popular misconceptions of Hell might lead to the question, "Will there be fun in Hell?" However, the Bible's description of Hell should lead us to consider the doctrine of Hell "with great sobriety and even tears, realizing it is what each of us deserves" (See p. 148).

May your study of this subject provide you with knowledge that you can share with others. There are many who do not know what they must do to avoid the final judgment that awaits all whose names are not written in the Lamb's Book of Life. Tell them that Hell is not fun. Nor is it inevitable. Instead, we can know for sure that we are going to Heaven! We can know with certainty that we will never see the fires of Hell nor be cast into its outer darkness.

LEARNING OBJECTIVES

- To learn the biblical doctrine of Hell.
- To learn what Scripture teaches us concerning the reality of Hell.
- To learn how Scripture describes Hell.
- To respond with head, heart, and will to the scriptural teaching and understanding of how we can avoid condemnation and pass from death unto life.

LEVEL ONE QUESTIONS

1. Given that Romans 3:10 says, "There is none righteous, no, not one," every person deserves to be judged worthy of spending all eternity in Hell. Whereas many people assume that by default they will go to Heaven when they die, the truth is that they will go to Hell unless, as John 5:24 says, "they shall not come into judgment, but have passed from death into life." What are some of the ways people try to avoid thinking about the subject of Hell? (See pp. 156-157.)

_____

_____

_____

"If we have never entered into a personal relationship with Jesus Christ (even though we may have been church members for years), then we have reason to fear Hell" (p. 158).

2. How should we respond to God's warning about Hell? (See pp. 157-158.)

_____

_____

_____

_____

3. More than any other person in Scripture, Jesus taught about the reality of Hell. How did He speak of it? (See p. 158.)

_____

_____

_____

_____

4. How is Hell described in the Bible? (See pp. 158-159.)

_____

_____

"Those who suppose that God is too loving to ever punish sin do not know the God who has revealed Himself in Scripture.... But those who realize that God is holy, and that man is depraved, his heart unclean, realize that their hope lies in the death and resurrection of Jesus Christ. For on a Cross outside the city wall of Jerusalem, the Son of God endured the wrath of His Father for those that would trust in Him" (pp. 159-160).

_____

_____

_____

_____

_____

_____

_____

_____

_____

"Our hope is simply this: Christ dies on a Cross and we who trust in Him may by His grace go to Heaven" (p. 152).

5. According to theologian A. A. Hodge, what do all the Church fathers, Reformers, biblical scholars, commentaries, and systematic theologies agree that the Scriptures teach concerning the "impenitent"? (See p. 159.)

_____

_____

_____

6. What are the two mistaken views that are used to argue against the eternal punishment of our sins in Hell? What truths do they ignore? (See pp. 159-160.)

_____

_____

_____

_____

7. What did Dr. Kennedy think was the only way people would come to appreciate the biblical teachings on Hell? (See p. 160.)

_____

_____

_____

_____

LEVEL TWO QUESTIONS

1. Before you read all the Scriptures describing Hell that are listed in this chapter, what did you think Hell was like?

_____

_____

_____

_____

2. What attitudes have you encountered about Hell in talking to your family or friends or fellow workers?

_____

_____

_____

_____

3. Do you now see more urgency in sharing the Good News that there is a way to avoid Hell? Do you want to share with others the fact that we can be sure we will go to Heaven when we die?

_____

_____

_____

_____

4. Read Revelation 20:11-15:

> Then I saw a great white throne and Him who sat on it, from whose face the earth and the heaven fled away. And there was found no place for them. And I saw the dead, small and great, standing before God, and books were opened. And another book was opened, which is the Book of Life. And the dead were judged according to their works, by the things which were written in the books. The sea gave up the dead who were in it, and Death and Hades delivered up the dead who were in them. And they were judged, each one according to his works. Then Death and Hades were cast into the lake of fire. This is the second death. And anyone not found written in the Book of Life was cast into the lake of fire.

What will be your hope on the day of God's final judgment? What do you want to tell others to prepare them for that day?

_____

_____

_____

_____

_____

_____

_____

_____

_____

_____

LEVEL THREE QUESTIONS

1. If you know for sure that your name is written in the Book of Life, you can pray for others, including your family members, friends, and co-workers who do not have that same comfort.

> Father, the great purity of Your Holiness stands in stark contrast to my sin. I know that I am not righteous. O God, this day may I behold the Lamb of God, who alone can take away my sins and make me righteous in Your sight. I pray for those in my family, my friends and fellow workers who have never confessed their need for a Savior from sin. Show them Your Son, the Lamb who was the perfect sacrifice for sin. Draw them to Him, that they may receive the gift of eternal life and forgiveness of sins, which only You can give. Open their hearts through Your Holy Spirit to respond to Christ's love poured out for sinners through His death on the Cross. He took the eternal punishment we deserve. In Christ's name I pray. Amen.

2. The following prayer is one you may want to share with family members, friends, or fellow workers who have come to realize their need to escape the judgment of God in Hell for their sins and to pass from death unto life:

> Heavenly Father, this day I embrace Your Son, Jesus Christ, as my personal Savior. I take into my own heart the One who came that I might live. I repent of my sins, which are beyond my counting. Therefore, by faith I claim and believe the promise that he that trusts in You shall not come into condemnation, but is passed from death unto life. I rejoice that by Your grace I shall never see the bottomless pit or experience the outer darkness. I thank You, Father, because now that I have taken Christ as my Savior, I shall, in the moment of death, be transported into Paradise to be with You forever and ever. Amen.

ANSWERS TO LEVEL ONE QUESTIONS

QUESTION 1: People may try to avoid thinking about Hell by:
a) dismissing the concept as "old-fashioned,"
b) claiming they believe in Heaven, but not Hell,
c) suppressing any thought of it because it is what they fear most.

QUESTION 2: We should respond to God's warning about Hell by turning to Christ in faith and entering into a personal relationship with Him. Then we will immediately be saved from the penalty of Hell, which is the punishment we justly deserve for our sins. John 3:18 assures us that "He who believes in Him is not condemned; but he who does not believe is condemned already, because he has not believed in the name of the only begotten Son of God.

QUESTION 3: When Jesus spoke of Hell, He didn't speak to frighten, but rather to warn people of the reality of it and to offer Himself as the alternative to Hell through trusting in Him as the Way, the Truth and the Life.

QUESTION 4: Hell is described in the Bible as:
a) Everlasting fire, prepared for the devil and his angels—see Matthew 25:41: "Then He will also say to those on the left hand, 'Depart from Me, you cursed, into the everlasting fire prepared for the devil and his angels.'"
b) Hell fire, where the worm does not die and the fire is not quenched—see Mark 9:47-48: "And if your eye causes you to sin, pluck it out. It is better for you to enter the kingdom of God with one eye, rather than having two eyes, to be cast into hell fire—where 'Their worm does not die, and the fire is not quenched.'"
c) The lake which burns with fire and brimstone—see Revelation 21:8: "But the cowardly, unbelieving, abominable, murderers, sexually immoral, sorcerers, idolaters, and all liars shall have their part in the lake which burns with fire and brimstone, which is the second death."
d) The bottomless pit—see Revelation 9:1-1: "Then the fifth angel sounded: And I saw a star fallen from heaven to the earth. To him was given the key to the bottomless pit."
e) Outer darkness—see Matthew 8:12: "But the sons of the kingdom will be cast out into outer darkness. There will be weeping and gnashing of teeth."
f) The place where there shall be wailing and gnashing of teeth—see Matthew 13:42: "...and will cast them into the furnace of fire. There will be wailing and gnashing of teeth."
g) A place where one cries, "I am tormented in this flame"—see Luke 16:24: "Then he cried and said, 'Father Abraham, have mercy on me, and send Lazarus that he may dip the tip of his finger in water and cool my tongue; for I am tormented in this flame.'"
h) A place where, as Revelation 14:11 states, "the smoke of their torment ascends forever and ever; and they have no rest day or night, who worship the beast and his image, and whoever receives the mark of his name."

QUESTION 5: According to the theologian A. A. Hodge, all the Church fathers, Reformers, biblical scholars, commentaries, and systematic theologies agree that the Scriptures teach that the "impenitent" will be eternally punished in Hell.

QUESTION 6: The two mistaken views that are used to argue against the eternal punishment of our sins in Hell are that: a) God is too loving to ever punish sin. This ignores His justice, holiness and righteousness. b) Man is too good for such a fate. This ignores man's totally sinful heart, which is deceitful above all things.

QUESTION 7: Dr. Kennedy thought the only way people come to truly appreciate the biblical teachings on Hell is to come to know in their hearts that they will never go there!

17

Heaven, the Life Hereafter

INTRODUCTION

How do you imagine Heaven? Streets of gold? A river of crystal? The Tree of Life? These images are familiar to us; yet in our greatest imaginations we can barely picture the marvelous glories and beauties of Heaven.

"God has created us for eternity. Yet most of us act as if He had created us merely for this life," wrote Dr. Kennedy in the opening of this chapter. Yet the material world around us "is too much with us." Not because we long for the fleeting beauties of nature, but because we find our thoughts are heavy with the cares of this world. We find it challenging to follow Paul's exhortation:

> ...Seek those things which are above, where Christ is, sitting at the right hand of God. Set your mind on things above, not on things on the earth. For you died, and your life is hidden with Christ in God. When Christ who is our life appears, then you also will appear with Him in glory.
>
> —Colossians 3:1-4

So as we look at what Scripture tells us of Heaven, let us lift our thoughts to things which are above. Let us sings songs of Heaven, and rejoice that because we know Jesus, we know for sure we will some day be in Heaven with Him. There we will enjoy all Heaven's beauties and glories. There will be nothing left to imagine!

> It has not yet been revealed what we shall be, but we know that when He is revealed, we shall be like Him, for we shall see Him as He is.
>
> —I John 3:2

LEARNING OBJECTIVES

- To learn what the Scripture teaches concerning Heaven.
- To respond with head, heart, and will to the scriptural teaching and understanding of Heaven.

LEVEL ONE QUESTIONS

1. Heaven is a major theme of Scripture, and the Bible mentions it 550 times by that name alone. What are some of the other names mentioned in the Bible in reference to Heaven?
(See p. 162.)

_____

_____

_____

_____

_____

"If Heaven is our home, if Heaven is our destination, if Heaven is the greatest thing that we can ever contemplate, how much time do we spend in thinking about it? It might be an indicator of whether or not we are going there—because those that are have a foretaste, an earnest, in their hearts now; and those that are not, probably never give it a thought" (p. 162).

2. Revelation 21:16–17 provides dimensions of the heavenly city. By modern calculations, how large would this city be? (See pp. 162-163.)

_____

_____

_____

3. What promise has Jesus given to us, which assures us that Heaven is a real place? (See pp. 162-163.)

_____

_____

_____

4. In addition to our hope of Heaven, what does Revelation 21:1 also tell us we can look forward to after Christ's return? (See p. 165.)

_____

_____

This earth will be purged by fire, reconstituted, glorified; and it seems that the dwelling place of the redeemed will be throughout the entire universe, which will be delivered from the bondage of sin at that time" (p. 165).

5. What will be our physical condition in the new Heaven and earth? (See p. 165.)

_____

_____

"If there is anything in this world that is deserving of human interest, it is the greatest thing man has ever conceived of: the Paradise of God. If people should be wholly taken up and their interest consumed with the pathetic things of earth, which are twisted and distorted with sin, how infinitely more interesting will be the new Heaven and the new earth" (p. 165).

6. What will our intellectual capacities be in the new Heaven and earth? (See p. 166.)

_____

_____

_____

7. What other benefits and blessings will we experience in the new Heaven and earth? (See pp. 166-167.)

_____

_____

_____

_____

8. What assurance can we have that we will go to Heaven? (See p. 169. See also chapter three.)

_____

_____

_____

_____

_____

"And that, my friends, is election or predestination: that God looked down from all eternity upon a world of sinners and decided to extend mercy to a vast number of people whom no one can number; and that in their appointed time He extended that mercy, not because of anything foreseen in them, but entirely and totally because of what God is—the God of all grace" (p. 32).

LEVEL TWO QUESTIONS

1. Would you consider yourself to be "heavenly minded?" How would you react if someone said to you, "You're so heavenly minded, you're no earthly good!"

_____

_____

_____

_____

2. What makes you long for Heaven? Is it the troubles of this earth, or the "joy inexpressible" that we will experience when we see Jesus? Consider the following verses:

> I Peter 1:7-9: "... that the genuineness of your faith, being much more precious than gold that perishes, though it is tested by fire, may be found to praise, honor, and glory at the revelation of Jesus Christ, whom having not seen you love. Though now you do not see Him, yet believing, you rejoice with joy inexpressible and full of glory, receiving the end of your faith—the salvation of your souls."
> I Peter 4:13: "... but rejoice to the extent that you partake of Christ's sufferings, that when His glory is revealed, you may also be glad with exceeding joy."

_____

_____

_____

_____

_____

_____

3. What are things you can do to "set your affections on things above?" (See Colossians 3:1-4.)

_____

_____

_____

4. Think of the last funeral you attended. Was it clear from the way the funeral was conducted that the person had a strong profession of faith in Christ Jesus? How did that impact you?

_____

_____

_____

5. What would you want your funeral to be like? Is that a difficult thing for you to plan or consider?

_____

_____

_____

6. Have you received the King of Heaven as the King of your heart?

_____

_____

_____

_____

LEVEL THREE QUESTIONS

1. Do you know family members or friends or fellow workers who are worried about whether or not they will go to Heaven when they die? If so, what could you share with them after your study of this chapter to encourage them to seek assurance through receiving Jesus Christ as the King of their heart?

_____

_____

_____

_____

_____

2. If you can say, as Dr. Kennedy did at the end of this chapter, "I am going to Heaven. This I know. I do not deserve it. I never have and never will. But by the pure, unmerited grace of God, through the Cross of Jesus Christ my Savior, I am going to Paradise forever—and ever—and ever—and ever." Write a prayer of praise and thanksgiving to the Lord for His marvelous gift of grace in your life.

_____

_____

_____

_____

_____

3. You can pray the following prayer for someone you love who is still walking in darkness and has not yet received the gift of eternal life.

> O Lord, I pray for _____ who is walking in darkness, staggering through the blackness of this world on the way to an eternal death. May _____ see his/her sin and hopelessness. May _____ look into the face of Christ upon the Cross and know that for this cause He came from Heaven; for this cause He laid aside His glory and became incarnate in human flesh. For us and for our sin He died that the penalty might be paid—that the gift of God, which is eternal life, might be given. Lord, may _____ this hour believe. May his/her heart cry out, "Lord Jesus, I open the door. Come with Your light and life and peace and joy. Come and bring with You Your Heaven. Dwell in my heart by faith. I receive You. I trust You. I commit myself unto You. Take me and make me Your own, that I may love You now and love You forevermore." In Your wonderful name alone I pray, Amen and Amen.

ANSWERS TO LEVEL ONE QUESTIONS

QUESTION 1: Some of the other names mentioned in the Bible in reference to Heaven are: a country; "a city which has foundations, whose builder and maker is God" (Hebrews 11:10); a house; a place prepared for us (John 14:2).

QUESTION 2: Revelation 21:16-17 provides dimensions of the heavenly city. By modern calculations this city would be 528 thousand stories high and 1 trillion, 188 billion square miles.

QUESTION 3: The promise Jesus has given to us, which assures us that Heaven is a real place, is John 14:2, "In My Father's house are many mansions; if it were not so, I would have told you. I go to prepare a place for you."

QUESTION 4: Revelation 21:1 tells us we can look forward to a new earth as well as a new Heaven.

QUESTION 5: In the new Heaven and earth we will have glorified bodies. Our senses will be enlarged greatly in their capacities, with our hearing and sight magnified to an extraordinary degree.

QUESTION 6: Our intellectual capacities in the new Heaven and earth will allow us to have the infinite continuous progress of knowledge. We will grow in wisdom and knowledge, even though we will be morally perfected. Although Adam, in his first state of innocence was without sin, he continued to grow in knowledge and was not omniscient.

HEAVEN, THE LIFE HEREAFTER

QUESTION 7: Other benefits and blessings of the new Heaven and earth include:

a) No more sorrow or sadness,

b) No pain or physical suffering,

c) No sin,

d) Pure and perfect love,

e) The outward and external beauties of the new Heaven and earth,

f) Eternal security and the never-ending enjoyment of all good forever,

g) Reunion with loved ones.

QUESTION 8: The assurance we have that we will go to Heaven is based in Scripture. I John 5:13 tells us, "These things I have written to you who believe in the name of the Son of God, that you may know that you have eternal life, and that you may continue to believe in the name of the Son of God." If we have believed in the name of Jesus Christ, the Son of God, and trusted in Him for our salvation, we can be assured that we will someday experience the beauties and joys of Heaven and see the incomparable loveliness of our beloved Savior and enjoy Him forever!

18

The Bible

INTRODUCTION

"O let me think the solemn thought, that this book is God's handwriting—that these words are God's! Let me look at its date; it is dated from the hills of Heaven. Let me look at its letters; they flash glory on my eye. Let me read the chapters; they are big with meaning and mysteries unknown. Let me turn over the prophecies; they are pregnant with unthought-of wonders. Oh, book of books! And wast thou written by my God? Then will I bow before thee."

— Charles Spurgeon

"The whole counsel of God concerning all things necessary for His own glory, man's salvation, faith and life, is either expressly set down in Scripture, or by good and necessary consequence may be deduced from Scripture: unto which nothing at any time is to be added, whether by new revelations of the Spirit, or traditions of men."

— The Westminster Confession of Faith, Chapter I, Article 6

"Hammer away, ye hostile hands, ye hammers break, God's anvil stands.
The word of the Lord endureth forever."

— Inscription on Huguenot Monument

LEARNING OBJECTIVES

- To learn what the Bible testifies concerning itself as the Word of God.
- To learn how we know that a prophet is sent from God.
- To learn what prophecies recorded in Scripture have been fulfilled that show the Bible is the Word of God.
- To respond with head, heart, and will to the scriptural teaching and understanding of the Bible as the Word of God.

LEVEL ONE QUESTIONS

1. The Bible explicitly and repeatedly claims to be the Word of God. Note how many times in the Old Testament we see the phrase, "Thus saith the Lord." What did Buddha and Confucius claim concerning their writings? What did Muhammad claim concerning the Koran? (See pp. 172-173.)

_____

_____

_____

2. What is the biblical test to see if a prophet is speaking the truth? (See pp. 174-175.)

_____

_____

_____

"The truth of God is living, vital, and life-transforming; and it is vitally important, especially in this day of confusion, this day of ignorance concerning the things of God, that Christian people be well established concerning the truth of God's Word" (p. 171).

3. Are there "predictive prophecies" in the writings of Buddha or Confucius? What is the character of the only prophecy of Muhammad that was fulfilled? What is the most significant prophecy of Jesus concerning Himself? (See p. 175.)

_____

_____

_____

_____

_____

"You say that you believe that the Bible is the Word of God. Is this simply some blind belief, some leap into darkness, some wish being the father to the thought? Or is there any substantive proof, any demonstration of the fact that the Bible is, indeed, the Word of God?" (p. 172).

4. In contrast to the several thousands of "specific, concrete, and definite" prophecies contained in Scriptures, what was the character of the prophecies of the Delphian Oracle and psychics like Jeane Dixon? (See p. 175.)

_____

_____

_____

_____

_____

_____

_____

5. How many specific prophecies concerning the life of Christ are found in the Old Testament? (See p. 176.)

_____

_____

_____

_____

6. The Bible also contains many prophecies concerning ancient cities and nations that bounded Israel. What specific kinds of events were prophesied concerning these cities and nations? (See p. 176.)

"How do you know that the Bible is the Word of God? That is a good question to face when we are approaching any branch of human learning. It is what is known as the epistemological question. It is the science of knowledge. How do you know that is the epistemological question? How do you know the Bible is the Word of God? How do you know that a prophet is sent from God? The Bible answers these questions very clearly" (p. 172).

_____

_____

_____

_____

_____

7. The ancient city of Tyre was the capital of much of the ancient world for two thousand years. Write the prophecy that the Lord directed Ezekiel to give against the city of Tyre. (See Ezekiel 26:4-5, 7, 12, 14.)

_____

_____

_____

_____

"...look at the fact that almost every major city and virtually every nation within a thousand miles of Israel had its entire future prophesied by the Bible. So these are prophecies so specific, so concrete, so definite, that anybody can tell whether they have been fulfilled" (p. 176).

8. Who finally fulfilled Ezekiel's prophecy and took the stones, timber, and soil of Tyre and placed them in the midst of the sea (Ezekiel 26:12)? How many years after the initial destruction of Tyre did this occur? (See pp. 177-178.)

_____

_____

_____

_____

9. The city of Samaria was the capital of the northern kingdom of Israel. What did the prophet Micah prophecy concerning it in Micah 1:5–6? What did Dr. Kennedy find when he visited the location of that city? (See pp. 179-180.)

_____

_____

_____

_____

"These are startling prophecies. They are exceedingly specific....Thus we will know that the Lord is God. The extent of the desolation both geographically and chronologically is described. Here is a bold gauntlet thrown down before unbelievers" (p. 181).

TRUTHS THAT TRANSFORM STUDY GUIDE

10. The prophecies concerning the land of Edom are very specific, as were the prophecies concerning Nineveh, Babylon, and Egypt. What common thread do you see running through the accounts that Dr. Kennedy provides of the fulfillment of these prophecies? (See pp. 180-192.)

_____

_____

_____

_____

11. When we started our study of *Truths That Transform*, we saw in Chapter One , "The Sovereignty of God," that God indeed controls the free acts of men. Sometimes history shows divine irony in the ways God uses men to carry out His purposes. Julian the Apostate, Emperor of Rome, tried to replace Christianity with paganism throughout the Roman Empire during the fourth century A.D. Yet God used him to carry out His sovereign plan. How? (See p. 187.)

_____

_____

_____

_____

"The Bible clearly points out that God controls the spirits of all those whom He has created. . . . 'the king's heart is in the hand of Jehovah as the rivers of water. He turneth it whithersoever He will.' A person's goings are established by Jehovah" (p. 13).

LEVEL TWO QUESTIONS

I. Have you ever had the opportunity to talk about comparisons between Christianity and various religions? In addition to what you learned in Chapter Five, "The Incomparable Christ," what have you learned about the Bible in this chapter that you could share with others?

_____

_____

_____

_____

_____

_____

> "There is not the slightest hint in the writings of Confucius that they are a divine revelation. He never dreamed of them as being such. Nor does Buddha claim for his writings any sort of divine revelation. So we see that in many of the great religions of the world no such claim is made; but over two thousand times in the Old Testament alone, the claim is made: 'Thus saith the Lord'" (pp. 172-173).

2. We often hear people say, "I don't believe the Bible is true. It is full of contradictions and errors." How would you respond? (See pp. 173-174.)

_____

_____

_____

_____

_____

_____

3. Most of us meet people daily who do not believe the Bible is truly God's Word. They have been told that science has disproved the Scriptures, or that the Bible contains a series of "myths." In this chapter, you have been given evidence of the specific literal fulfillment of numerous prophecies. Do you think that committing the details of one or two of these examples to memory would help you be better equipped to respond to those who attack the divine inspiration of the Scriptures? (I Peter 3:15).

_____

_____

_____

_____

"But sanctify the Lord God in your hearts, and always be ready to give a defense to everyone who asks you a reason for the hope that is in you, with meekness and fear" (I Peter 3:15).

4. How has your study of this chapter on "The Bible" transformed your view of the Bible as God's Word?

_____

_____

_____

_____

_____

LEVEL TWO QUESTIONS

I. Paul exhorted the Christians at Corinth:

> "Therefore, having these promises, beloved, let us cleanse ourselves from all
> filthiness of the flesh and spirit, perfecting holiness in the fear of God."
> —2 Corinthians 7:1

After completing this study of *Truths That Transform*, may you be able to offer praise and thanksgiving to God and pray the following prayer:

> Lord, I have seen Your faithfulness to keep Your Word in every detail.
> Fill me with Your Holy Spirit and cleanse me from all filthiness of the flesh
> and spirit. Perfect me in holiness and in reverence and respect for You
> in all your sovereignty, might, and power. Truly great and marvelous are
> Your works, Lord God Almighty! Just and true are Your ways, O King of
> the saints! Amen.

If there is one overall goal that this study has sparked in your heart and mind, please write it below.

_____

_____

_____

_____

_____

_____

> "Therefore, my beloved brethren, be steadfast, immovable, always abounding in
> the work of the Lord, knowing that your labor is not in vain in the Lord."
> —I Corinthians 15:58

ANSWERS TO LEVEL ONE QUESTIONS

QUESTION 1: Neither Buddha nor Confucius claimed that their writings were divine revelation. Muhammad did claim that his god Allah revealed the Koran to him.

QUESTION 2: The biblical test to see if a prophet is speaking the truth is found in Deuteronomy 18:22: "When a prophet speaks in the name of the LORD, if the thing does not happen or come to pass, that is the thing which the LORD has not spoken; the prophet has spoken it presumptuously; you shall not be afraid of him."

QUESTION 3: There are no "predictive prophecies" in the writings of Buddha or Confucius. The only prophecy of Muhammad that was fulfilled was his "self-fulfilling prophecy" that he would return to Mecca. The most significant prophecy of Jesus concerning Himself that was fulfilled was that He would rise again from the dead on the third day.

QUESTION 4: In contrast to the several thousands of "specific, concrete, and definite" prophecies contained in the Scriptures, the prophecies of the Delphian Oracle were ambiguous riddles that could be interpreted more than one way, and the psychic Jeane Dixon, the twentieth century psychic, made numerous predictions that were never fulfilled.

QUESTION 5: There are 333 specific prophecies concerning the life of Christ to be found in the Old Testament. For an in-depth look at this subject, see Dr. Kennedy's book, *Messiah: Prophecies Fulfilled*. The following is a short excerpt from Dr. Kennedy's sermon, "Prophecies Concerning the Messiah."

> The Old Testament contains 333 prophecies concerning the coming of Christ, which include 456 specific facts or details concerning the Messiah that was to come. All of these prophecies were written between 400 B.C. and 1400 B.C....
>
> In a book, *The Case for Jesus the Messiah*, by Ankerberg, Weldon, and Kaiser, we are told that Professor Peter Stoner, Professor Emeritus of Science at Westmont College, examined the probabilities of just eight of these prophecies coming to pass. He said the probability would be one in 10^{17} power.
>
> What does that mean? Since we are not used to dealing with figures like that, he tried to make it simple for us by saying that if you were to mark a silver dollar; put it in with enough silver dollars to cover the state of Texas, two feet thick; then have a blind man walk around the state, back and forth, up and down, every which way for thousands of miles until finally he decides to stop at a place of his choice—reach down, dig around in the silver dollars, and pull out one of them—the chance of his finding that marked silver dollar is equal to the chance of only eight of those prophecies coming to pass.

If that doesn't boggle your mind enough, Stoner also "computed the probability of 48 prophecies being fulfilled in one person as 10^{157}. How large is 10^{157}? 10^{157} contains 157 zeros!" ... Nobel prize-winning scientists have pointed out that if anything has a chance less than 10^{50}, "the probabilities are so small, it is impossible to think they will ever occur," even cosmically.

So you can see that the chance of these prophecies being fulfilled are infinitely far beyond the possibility of their being due to chance or simply an accidental occurrence.

QUESTION 6: The Bible contains prophecies concerning ancient cities and nations that bounded Israel which included specific details concerning:
a) Cities or nations that would be destroyed and never again inhabited.
b) Cities whose inhabitants would be killed, but the city would continue to exist.
c) Cities whose base would be diminished, but they would continue to exist over the centuries.

QUESTION 7: The ancient city of Tyre was the capital of the ancient world for two thousand years. The prophecy that the Lord directed Ezekiel to give against the city of Tyre is found in Ezekiel 26.
Ezekiel 26:4-5: "And they shall destroy the walls of Tyre and break down her towers; I will also scrape her dust from her, and make her like the top of a rock. 'It shall be a place for spreading nets in the midst of the sea, for I have spoken,' says the Lord God; 'it shall become plunder for the nations.'"
Ezekiel 26:7: "For thus says the Lord God: 'Behold, I will bring against Tyre from the north Nebuchadnezzar king of Babylon, king of kings, with horses, with chariots, and with horsemen, and an army with many people.'"
Ezekiel 26:12: "They will plunder your riches and pillage your merchandise; they will break down your walls and destroy your pleasant houses; they will lay your stones, your timber, and your soil in the midst of the water."
Ezekiel 26:14: "I will make you like the top of a rock; you shall be a place for spreading nets, and you shall never be rebuilt, for I the Lord have spoken,' says the Lord God."

QUESTION 8: Ezekiel's prophecy was fulfilled when Alexander the Great took the stones, timber, and soil of the destroyed mainland city of Tyre and placed them in the midst of the sea to build a bridge to reach out to the fortified island city of Tyre in order to conquer it. This took place two and a half centuries after Ezekiel wrote his prophecy. Today it has become "scraped clean" and like a rock, and tourists will find the fishermen drying their nets on the rock of Tyre.

QUESTION 9: The city of Samaria was the capital of the northern kingdom of Israel.
Micah prophesied, as recorded in Micah 1:5-6:

> All this is for the transgression of Jacob
> And for the sins of the house of Israel.
> What is the transgression of Jacob?

Is it not Samaria?
And what are the high places of Judah?
Are they not Jerusalem?
"Therefore I will make Samaria a heap of ruins in the field,
Places for planting a vineyard;
I will pour down her stones into the valley,
And I will uncover her foundations."

When Dr. Kennedy visited the location of that city, he saw the huge boulders that had been the walls of the city cast down into a deep valley and the foundations of the city exposed by excavations.

QUESTION 10: Throughout all of the accounts provided in this chapter regarding fulfillment of the specific prophecies concerning the land of Edom, the cities of Nineveh and Babylon, and the land of Egypt, the common thread one can see is the fact that each detailed prophecy has specifically been fulfilled in accordance with the biblical prophecy.

QUESTION 11: God used Julian the Apostate, Emperor of Rome, to carry out His sovereign plan, when he utterly destroyed the remaining wall of Babylon, thus completing the fulfillment of God's prophecy against one of the greatest enemies of Israel.

How to Lead a
Truths That Transform
Study Group

After completing this study as an individual, you may wish to use it in the context of a small group study or Sunday school class. The individual study format can easily be adapted to a format that is suitable for these settings. The questions provided in this Study Guide can facilitate group discussion of the material as well as prompt further discussion of personal reflection and application of the biblical truths taught in each chapter.

PREPARING TO LEAD

Your success as a group leader is not dependent on your knowing more about the topic than the members of the study group. However, there are several things you can do to ensure that those who are studying *Truths That Transform* with you will benefit from this study to the greatest degree. We encourage you to prepare to lead by:

- Praying for the individual members who will be joining the study group.
- Praying for yourself and asking God to guide you in your preparation and your leadership.
- Praying for the study group to be united and for members to be willing to share openly with one another.
- Reading the chapters in *Truths That Transform* and preparing your answers to the Study Guide questions in advance.
- Planning your study group time—using the format provided below as a basic outline.

KEYS TO A SUCCESSFUL GROUP STUDY

Each member of the group should read the *Truths That Transform* chapter to be discussed and answer the Study Guide questions before the group meeting. If the group as a whole is prepared, the discussions will be more meaningful. Participants will have an understanding of the material and will have spent some time in reflecting on their personal application of it. Thus, the group discussions can be a time of greater learning from one another.

Also, members of the group should be willing to discuss and share their personal responses to the Level Two and Three Questions. These questions are intended to prompt deeper thinking about the personal application of these truths. There must be a level of trust for group members to willingly share such personal responses. Using smaller break-out groups of four or five members will provide a setting for this trust to develop over time. Ideally, these small groups should stay the same from week to week. Time should be allowed for the group members to pray for one another and to report the actions they have taken in response to the Level Three Questions.

DISCUSSION FACILITATES LEARNING

A format for group study that provides opportunity for interaction and exchange of personal insights provides an ideal way to deepen personal understanding. Discussion of the material in a small group setting is one of the best ways to develop greater confidence in one's ability to talk about the topics in everyday conversational settings. In this group study format, the leader serves as a guide and facilitator for the discussion of the chapter topic which has, in a sense, been "taught" by Dr. Kennedy in the book. The Study Guide questions can be used to prompt discussion of the chapter topics at several levels.

A discussion of the Level One Questions will provide a good review and overview of the chapter material. Whatever the size of your group, discussing the Level One Questions as a group allows people to ask questions and share their insights on the material. Before moving to the Level Two and Level Three Questions, however, the participants should move into their smaller break-out groups. These small groups allow each participant more opportunity to talk and share personal responses to these questions. This will increase each individual's learning and retention of the material. It is a simple principle of learning that we tend to remember more of what we say than what we hear! By providing the maximum opportunity for group members to discuss their personal responses to the topical material, you will increase the personal benefit each group member will derive from the study.

FORMAT FOR A STUDY GROUP SESSION
OPEN WITH PRAYER: Pray for the study group members to be transformed by the truths they will be learning in the session.

INVITE DISCUSSION OF THE STUDY GUIDE INTRODUCTION: Use the introduction example to generate discussion from the group, including additional examples or comments on the introductory material. Encourage expression of personal reactions and responses.[1]

DISCUSS THE LEVEL ONE QUESTIONS: This can be done with the entire group, primarily with the goal of reviewing the material, since answers to the Level One questions are provided in the Study Guide itself. There may be questions that arise at this point, which will trigger discussion. Some may want to comment on the material. You can encourage this to some degree, but you should watch the time so that there will be sufficient time for the small break-out groups to discuss the Level Two and Three Questions. If the discussion carries on too long, you can instruct the group to move into their smaller groups and continue it there.

SMALL BREAK-OUT GROUPS DISCUSS LEVEL TWO AND THREE QUESTIONS: During the first meeting, groups should be identified. Allowing people to select their own group will strengthen the bond within the group. You may want to explain beforehand that the groups will, in most cases, remain the same throughout the entire study. The primary purpose of the break-out groups is to allow everyone to talk and share their responses to the questions and to pray for one another and encourage each other to carry out the actions they have identified in response to the Level Three Questions.

ALLOW TIME FOR SMALL GROUPS TO PRAY: Approximately ten minutes before the end of the study session, encourage the small groups to spend the remaining time in prayer.

CONCLUDE THE SESSION: Thank everyone for their participation and end with prayer for the entire group.

CONCLUSION

If you decide to lead a group study of *Truths That Transform*, be assured that the effort you invest in leading this study will be richly rewarded.[2] These truths are truly "life-changing scriptural truths." By assisting others to gain a deeper understanding of them you will be aiding them in their growth in the grace and knowledge of our Lord and Savior Jesus Christ. To Him be the glory both now and forever!

---

[1] If one of the responses is negative or critical, do not try to respond or "defend" the material. Thank the person for sharing and state that there will be opportunity to discuss these issues in more detail later. Do not allow one person's negative comment to dominate the group's study of the material. Later, when the smaller break-out groups have begun their discussion of the Level Two and Three Questions, you may visit this member's group to address his or her question in that context. Whenever possible, try to refer these questions directly back to the material in *Truths That Transform*. The more thoroughly you have prepared, the better you will be able to respond to questions from group members that may arise during the study session.

[2] We would appreciate your sending any comments regarding your use of this Study Guide in personal or group study to: discipleship@crministries.org.

NOTES

NOTES